CAMBRIDGE TEXTS IN THE HISTORY OF POLITICAL THOUGHT

JEAN BODIN

On Sovereignty

CAMBRIDGE TEXTS IN THE HISTORY OF POLITICAL THOUGHT

The series is intended to make available to students the most important texts required for an understanding of the history of political thought. The scholarship of the present generation has greatly expanded our sense of the range of authors indispensable for such an understanding, and the series will reflect those developments. It will also include a number of less well-known works, in particular those needed to establish the intellectual contexts that in turn help to make sense of the major texts. The principal aim, however, will be to produce new versions of the major texts themselves, based on the most up-to-date scholarship. The preference will always be for complete texts, and a special feature of the series will be to complement individual texts, within the compass of a single volume, with subsidiary contextual material. Each volume will contain an introduction on the historical identity and contemporary significance of the text concerned.

For a list of titles published in the series, please see end of book

JEAN BODIN

On Sovereignty

Four chapters from *The Six Books of the Commonwealth*

EDITED AND TRANSLATED BY

JULIAN H. FRANKLIN
Department of Political Science
Columbia University
New York, USA

CAMBRIDGE UNIVERSITY PRESS
CAMBRIDGE
NEW YORK PORT CHESTER
MELBOURNE SYDNEY

Published by the Press Syndicate of the University of Cambridge
The Pitt Building, Trumpington Street, Cambridge CB2 1RP
40 West 20th Street, New York, NY 10011–4211, USA
10 Stamford Road, Oakleigh, Victoria 3166, Australia

First published 1992

Printed in Great Britain by The Bath Press, Avon

A cataloguing in publication record for this book is available from the British Library

Library of Congress cataloguing in publication data

Bodin, Jean, 1530–1596.
[Six livres de la République. Selections. English]
On sovereignty: four chapters from six books of the commonwealth
/ Jean Bodin; edited and translated by Julian H. Franklin.
p. cm. – (Cambridge texts in the history of political
thought)
Translation of selections from Six livres de la République.
Includes bibliographical references and index.
ISBN 0 521 34206 6 (hardback). ISBN 0 521 34992 3 (paperback)
1. Sovereignty. 2. Political science – Early works to 1800.
I. Franklin, Julian H. II. Title. III. Series.
JC327.B662513 1992
320.1'5 – dc20 91–19029 CIP

ISBN 0 521 34206 6 hardback
ISBN 0 521 34992 3 paperback

To the memory of my mother, Molly Franklin

Contents

Acknowledgments

I owe a lot to many friends and colleagues who contributed at one point or another to my work on Bodin. But I should like to give special thanks here for the help I received on this particular project. My wife, Paula A. Franklin, edited the entire manuscript with unerring watchfulness and good taste. Raymond Geuss and Quentin Skinner, editors of this series, were generous with their time and made a number of useful suggestions for the Introduction. A translation grant from The National Endowment for the Humanities for the academic year 1989–90 helped to make the whole project feasible.

Introduction

An outline of Bodin's career

Jean Bodin (1529/30–1596) was born at Angers into a modestly successful middle-class family. He entered the Carmelite order in 1545 and seemed destined for a career in the Church. But in 1548–49 he obtained release from his vows, apparently on the grounds that he had been too young at the time he professed them. For some time, indeed, he seems to have been moving in other directions. Having gone in 1547 to the Carmelite house in Paris, he managed to pursue studies at the royal Collège de quatre langues, and by the time he left Paris, around 1550, he had acquired a truly formidable humanist education. He was to become one of the foremost polyhistors of his period. By this time he had also become engaged in a private search for religious truth which was to put him under suspicion of heresy at many points in his career. He was probably charged with heresy in 1547, and may have escaped punishment only by recanting. But the evidence for a public conversion to Calvinism in the early 1550s is indecisive and is generally discounted.

Throughout the 1550s, Bodin was a student of law at the University of Toulouse where he also served as a teaching assistant. In the later Renaissance, and in France more than any other place in Europe, academic jurisprudence had become closely linked to humanist erudition, and Bodin was strongly attracted to it. But by the end of the decade in Toulouse, his hopes for an academic career were disappointed. He was unable to obtain a professorship, and was unsuccessful also in his attempt to promote a new humanist college for the youth of the city. Around 1561, accordingly, he returned to

Paris as a barrister in Parlement. But Bodin's public career was always subordinate to an encyclopedic program of research and writing, projected in his early years. His *Methodus ad facilem historiarum cognitionem*, a guide to the study of universal history, appeared in 1566. In 1568 he published *La response à M. Malestroit*, which attributed the price revolution of the period to the influx of bullion from America. Despite anticipations by Copernicus, it was the first elaboration of the quantity theory of money from the standpoint of political economy. As a result of such writings, as well as his broad erudition and a gift for conversation, Bodin became something of a public figure.

By the end of the 1560s, he had come to the attention of high personages at the royal court. Around 1570, he was entrusted by the king, Charles IX, with a number of administrative and political missions; his company was sought by Henry III who became king in 1574; and in 1571 he entered the service of Francis, duke of Alençon, the youngest of the princes of the blood, and next in line to the throne after Henry III, who could not have children. As counsellor and master of requests to Alençon, Bodin not only had excellent long-term prospects, but also became directly involved in much of the intrigue and diplomacy of the time. But the high point of his prospects came with the publication in 1576 of his *Six livres de la république*.* This was a systematic exposition of French and universal public law, unprecedented in its scope and depth, which developed an absolutist theory of royal sovereignty while still accommodating a great many traditional restraints on the practice of governance. Coming at a dark period in the French religious wars, this account was welcomed in enlightened sections of the French political elite, and the *République* won almost instantaneous acclaim. In 1576, Bodin also contracted an advantageous marriage. His future thus appeared assured.

There now occurred, however, an unfortunate confrontation with the government. In 1576, Bodin was chosen as a deputy for the Third Estate of Vermandois to the Estates-General of Blois. As all kings did at all Estates, Henry III urgently requested new taxation, and sought to make it popular by promising to use the revenues to enforce religious uniformity. Bodin, as an enlightened royalist, was opposed to civil war and saw only a calamitous new burden for an already overtaxed Third Estate. By dogged and courageous opposition, he turned

*The accent on 'république' will be supplied in all cases in accordance with modern usage.

the Third against the king's proposals, and also prevailed against various stratagems of the government designed to override the Third Estate's refusal. This stance, as we shall see, was not inconsistent with recognition, as Bodin understood it, of the king's absolute authority. But it cost him the favor of the court and the high office of royal master of requests to which he had expected an appointment.

In 1577, Bodin published an account of the Estates of Blois and also an answer to early critics of his *République*. In 1580, he published his distressing and all too influential book on demonology, *De la démonomanie des sorciers*, in which he described at great length the passion of witches for evil forces and the way by which they should be detected and punished. In 1581, he was sent to England to help advance the duke of Alençon's continuing matrimonial suit with Elizabeth I; a year later he accompanied the duke to Antwerp, where the latter made yet another unsuccessful attempt to get a crown. But with the death of the duke in 1584, Bodin's involvement in high politics was over. He had already left Paris for Laon, the seat of his wife's family. There he succeeded to the post of king's attorney on the death of his brother-in-law in 1587. Bodin remained at Laon in that capacity until his death in 1596.

This was not a happy time for Bodin. After the assassination of Henry III in 1589, a new phase of civil war broke out over succession to the throne. The then Protestant Henry of Navarre (King Henry IV), whose claim to the throne was the stronger under French law, was opposed by Cardinal Charles of Bourbon, who was recognized as King Charles X by the Catholic party. Bodin at Laon was now in a difficult position. The town came under the control of the revolutionary Catholic League which dominated its political life until Laon was taken by Henry in 1594. The League negated all the principles of legitimacy, non-resistance, and toleration with which Bodin had been associated. But like many other royalist magistrates of the time, Bodin collaborated. He was presumably driven by fear of losing his office and his property, and perhaps his life as well, since once again he was under suspicion of heresy. Only in 1594 did he come forward for Henry of Navarre.

Although dreary politically, these last years at Laon were highly productive intellectually. During this period, Bodin published two relatively short pieces on ethics. His massive system of natural philosophy, the *Universae naturae theatrum*, appeared posthumously in

1596, the year of Bodin's death. But the most remarkable achievement of this period was his extraordinary work on religion, the manuscript of which was completed in 1593. The *Colloquium heptaplomeres* is a series of conversations among a proponent of natural religion, a philosophical skeptic, a Jew, a Muslim, a Catholic, a Lutheran, and a Zwinglian on the nature of the true religion, in which all of the historical religions are portrayed as deviations from an original natural religion that is still knowable by speculative reason. For obvious reasons, the book could not be published in Bodin's lifetime, and the first complete edition came only in 1857. Throughout the seventeenth and eighteenth centuries, however, manuscript copies of the *Colloquium heptaplomeres* circulated among the European philosophical elite.

Bodin, as we have indicated, was a religious maverick who may have gone through several phases before reaching his mature position. Given various things he said (and failed to say) on religious subjects, Bodin was very early taken as a Judaizer. And that is now a well-established scholarly opinion. The treatment of the spokesman for Judaism in the *Colloquium heptaplomeres*, the character of his ethical reflections, an episode reported in *La démonomanie des sorciers* – as well as certain indications that go back even earlier – all point to a kind of Judaizing neo-Platonism as Bodin's personal and private religion. Outwardly, however, he remained a Catholic, and on his death, in accordance with his will, he was buried as a Catholic.

Bodin's theory of sovereignty

The four chapters rendered here from Jean Bodin's *Six livres de la république* constitute a relatively small portion of a massive treatise on public law and policy. But it is in these chapters above all that Bodin worked out his analysis of sovereignty which informed his thinking on the state and made the *République* a celebrated work. Bodin's account of sovereignty was a major event in the development of European political thought. His precise definition of supreme authority, his determination of its scope, and his analysis of the functions that it logically entailed, helped turn public law into a scientific discipline. And his elaboration of the implications of sovereignty through a systematic study of comparative public law helped launch a whole new literary genre, which in the seventeenth century was taken up not only in France and Spain, but in Germany as well.

Bodin's account of sovereignty, however, was also the source of confusion that helped prepare the way for the theory of royal absolutism, for he was primarily responsible for introducing the seductive but erroneous notion that sovereignty is indivisible. It is true, of course, that every legal system, by its very definition as an authoritative method of resolving conflicts, must rest upon some ultimate legal norm or rule of recognition which is the guarantee of coherence. But when Bodin spoke about the unity of sovereignty, the power he had in mind was not the constituent authority of the general community or the ultimate coordinating rule that the community had come to recognize, but the power, rather, of the ordinary agencies of government. He advanced, in other words, a theory of ruler sovereignty. His celebrated principle that sovereignty is indivisible thus meant that the high powers of government could not be shared by separate agents or distributed among them, but all had instead to be entirely concentrated in a single individual or group.

This thesis was controversial even as applied to the more consolidated kingships of France, Spain, and England, and it was hopelessly at odds with the constitution of the German Empire and other monarchies of central Europe and Scandinavia. Yet so seductive was the idea of indivisibility that it remained a celebrated issue among academic jurists for at least a half-century after Bodin wrote.[1]

The idea that concentration of power in the ruler is an essential condition of the state as such might seem at first sight to be deliberately absolutist, and Bodin, when he published the final version of his political doctrine in 1576, indeed argued that the king of France had all the power that a government could legitimately exercise, and that apparent restraints on royal power were not constitutional requirements, but mere recommendations of prudence and good government. Yet the earlier history of Bodin's thought suggests a somewhat different starting point. In his *Methodus ad facilem historiarum cognitionem* (1566), Bodin was not an absolutist, or was at least evasive on that subject, and his interest in the theory of sovereignty was clearly technical and quasi-academic.[2]

In the earliest phase of his professional career as an aspiring teacher at the law school of Toulouse, Bodin had apparently undertaken to identify those powers of a sovereign that could not also be held as a right of office by ordinary magistrates.[3] To say that a magistrate "held" or "had" a power by his right of office had been taken, by most medieval jurists, to mean that he could exercise that power according to his own discretion and without direct reliance on the king, so long as he remained within whatever legal limits might apply. Not all powers were, or needed to be, held this way, of course. The public officer might be acting solely on delegated power subject to immediate control. But by medieval notions, such an officer was little better than a servant. High officers of state, who exercised some degree of *merum*, or "pure" *imperium*, held their *imperium* by right. And since the *merum imperium* could include very high powers of the state, this conception of the right of office was naturally associated with a decentralized administration.[4]

With the growing consolidation of power in the French and other Renaissance monarchies, this view of office was increasingly attacked, most strenuously of all by Andrea Alciato, the great Italian legal humanist of the early sixteenth century. He held that the possession of *merum imperium* by right of office was a corruption of Roman civil law, and that every power in the state, other than (abusive) feudal grants, was merely a right of exercise derived by delegation from the prince.[5] This opinion was obviously favorable to royal power; and given Bodin's constant preference for strong monarchical authority, one might have expected him to welcome Alciato's view.

But Bodin was also an erudite and cautious legal craftsman who attempted, throughout his career, to reconcile the new idea of royal dominance with the French juridical tradition of which he was a great admirer and connoisseur. Against Alciato, accordingly, Bodin held that by the customary rule of public law in France, high magistrates could hold the *merum imperium* by right of office at least to the extent of imposing capital punishment. But against the medieval exponents of this view, he did not include those prerogatives that could make the magistrate a partner or rival of his prince. These could not be "held," but could be exercised by delegation only.[6]

Unlike Alciato and his followers, Bodin divided the *merum imperium* into a (minor) part that could be held by magistrates, and a (major) part held only by the prince.[7] By this conservative route he was led, ironically, to a new and theoretically momentous question as to the character of sovereignty. He now sought to determine those powers that could not be held by magistrates, but only exercised, if the prince was to be accounted sovereign. Although this topic had sometimes been touched upon by other jurists of the time, Bodin was to treat the question in a more fundamental and systematic way than anyone before him. He now proceeded to derive the necessary prerogatives, or "marks," of sovereignty from the concept of supremacy itself. The question that he asked, in other words, was what prerogatives a political authority must hold exclusively if it is not to acknowledge a superior or equal in its territory.

Bodin's first reflections on this question almost surely date back to his early career as an academic jurist at the University of Toulouse (which he left in 1559 after failing to secure a permanent appointment). But the scope and depth of his investigation was decisively shaped by a far-reaching methodological commitment that carried him well beyond the conventional approach to legal studies. Sometime around the end of his period in Toulouse, Bodin concluded that issues of legal theory could not be settled in the traditional fashion of the medieval civil lawyers by appeal to Roman norms alone. The use of high philological technique in the study of the Roman law by the great French school of legal humanism had prepared the way for a methodological revolution in which Bodin became a leading figure. The humanists, rejecting the medieval style of scholastic exegesis, had attempted to get back to the original meaning of the Roman texts, and to recover the underlying system of the *Corpus Juris*. But the further they went, the more critical they became of Roman law itself. The *Corpus Juris*, to list their main complaints, seemed incomplete in many areas, and most especially in public law; Justinian had often been cryptic and inaccurate in representing the best of Roman legal thought; many rules, some of which seemed basic to the system, were peculiar to the Roman state and obsolete for France; the *Corpus Juris* had not been arranged as a logically coherent system, and could not be reduced to one because of its defects and omissions. The intellectual authority of Roman law was thereby shaken, and this had a number of important repercussions.[8]

One of these was a new appreciation of domestic legal custom.[9] But an additional motif, especially strong in Bodin, was the idea of remedying deficiencies in the system of Roman law by consulting the materials of universal history.[10] This, in large part, was the theme of his *Methodus ad facilem historiarum cognitionem* (1566). The only way, says Bodin in the preface, to construct a truly universal legal science is to compare "all the laws of all, or the most famous, states and to select the best variety." A few years earlier, perhaps while he was still at Toulouse, he had produced a grandiose design for this comparison with his *Juris universi distributio*, or *Subdivisions of Law in its Entirety*; and the *Methodus*, or *Method for the Easy Comprehension of History*, presented a preliminary statement of his findings for the area of public law in its very lengthy chapter 6.

In this fashion, an enterprise that very likely started as an inquiry into the specific prerogatives of the ancient Roman emperors and the kings of France was transformed into a study of sovereignty in every kind of state. In Bodin's design, the basis for comparing states, and explaining their schemes of public law, was to determine and describe the locus of sovereignty in each. It thus required him to work out common principles of sovereignty that would apply to democracies and aristocracies as well as monarchies, and to variants of each of these in different times and places.

One consequence of this was a comprehensive and general definition of the rights of sovereignty. The *Corpus Juris* offered virtually nothing on the theory of public powers since it was primarily a scheme of private law. And the lists of regalian powers taken from feudal law were mere catalogues of particular privileges. In Bodin's *Methodus*, however, the essential rights are distinguished and reduced to five:

> And so having compared the arguments of Aristotle, Polybius, Dionysius [of Halicarnassus], and the jurists – with each other and with the universal history of commonwealths – I find that supremacy in a commonwealth consists of five parts. The first and most important is appointing magistrates and assigning each one's duties; another is ordaining and repealing laws; a third is declaring and terminating war; a fourth is the right of hearing appeals from all magistrates in last resort; and the last is the power of life and death where the law itself has made no provision for flexibility or clemency.[11]

This classification is not quite as modern as it seems. It becomes clear in the *République* that Bodin thinks of the legislative power (which he now puts first among the rights of sovereignty) as a very general power to command, so that it implicitly includes all others. It comprises not only the ordinary power to make law, but also what in modern usage would be called the constituent power, or right to change the constitution. The abeyance of this distinction, as we shall see, is costly. Yet Bodin makes a very important, and even decisive, step towards an adequate typology of public powers.

A second consequence of Bodin's comparative enterprise was his celebrated claim that sovereignty is indivisible, which he seems to have come to only at this point. In seeking to determine the form of state for ancient Rome and certain other classical republics traditionally reputed to be mixed, Bodin was finally led to ask, in strictly juridical terms, where the locus of sovereignty was to be found in a mixed constitution – in a constitution, that is, wherein the sovereign was said to be compounded of monarchy, aristocracy, and democracy, or any two of these.

Thus put, the question was completely new, since Polybius, and other exponents of the mixed constitution, thought of it more as a balance of effective influence than as a legal formula for partnership in sovereignty. Bodin's answer was that, beyond monarchy, aristocracy, and democracy – three simple forms of state – "no fourth had existed, or could even be imagined."[12] The difficulty with a mixed constitution, in other words, was not merely prudential or political. As Bodin saw it, the unity of a legal system seemed logically to require the unification of power in a single ruler or single ruling group.

This opinion is, of course, mistaken. Apart from federal decentralization, which I leave aside for the purpose of this Introduction,* a constitution can be mixed either by sharing, or by distribution. Where sovereignty is shared, the outcome is a compound polyarchy, the members of which, each retaining its identity within the whole, are the king, the senate, and the people, or any two of these, who may participate with different weights in any given governmental function. The idea of such a compound is not always easy to imagine.† The President of the United States, for example, is, by

*Bodin considers confederacies in Book I, chapter 7, and, as might be expected, denies that they constitute unified political systems.

†But it was clearly understood by Christoph Besold, one of the earliest and most incisive critics of the thesis of indivisibility. Answering Daniel Otto, a German follower of Bodin, he writes: "It is never possible, he [Otto] says, either in nature or even in imagination, for supreme authority, or majesty, to be shared with an inferior and still remain supreme. It remains supreme, I answer, but not in one individual. It is rather in the whole body, or corporation, of those who rule (*archonton*), but in such a way that it is not distributed equally among the parts. The prince will be conceded some large degree of eminence (which will be larger, of course, than what the Doge has in the Venetian commonwealth) or else it will be an aristocracy" (1626, p. 212). For debates on indivisibility in this period, see Franklin, "Sovereignty and the Mixed Constitution."

virtue of his veto, a member of the legislature along with the two houses of Congress. Yet it is hard to imagine an act of legislation as the "will" of such a complex entity, and more normal to think of it as an act of Congress subject, within certain limits, to approval by the President.

Where the constitutional principles of mixture are well understood, this way of speaking does not lead to theoretical confusion. But in the sixteenth century, the mixed constitution had not yet been explored juridically, and where it occurred, it was the legacy of traditional restraints and *ad hoc* adaptations that were not reflected in the legal terminology. In the limited monarchies of Europe, the king was still addressed as sovereign even though he might require the consent of the Estates or other body for the conduct of some of his affairs, and commentators on the ancient Roman republic often passed over periods in which the Senate exerted a legislative veto.

Hence jurists of the sixteenth century were readily misled. The mixed systems of their own time, or of the past, were hard to grasp as authentic partnerships in sovereignty, while the mixtures they imagined and triumphantly proved to be impossible were irrelevant. Bodin, for example, assumes that the only sense in which a constitution might be mixed by sharing would be to give each of the partners the entirety of power simultaneously, which is, of course, juridically absurd.

> But to institute the dominion of one, together with that of the few, and also with that of the many, simultaneously, is not only impossible but cannot even be imagined. For if sovereignty is by its nature indivisible, as we have shown above, how can it be allotted to one and to all at the same time? The first mark of sovereignty is to give law to all in general and to each in particular, and to command them. But will the citizens yield to being bound against their will when they, in turn, are empowered to coerce the person who commands them? If they willingly obey their majesty collapses; and yet if both parties refuse to be commanded, and there is no one obeying or commanding, it will be anarchy rather than a commonwealth, which is worse than the cruelest tyranny.*

*This is from the Latin version of 1586 (*De republica*, II, 1, p. 176). The French version, going back to 1576, describes the outcome as democracy, presumably on the grounds that all participate. But the possibility of contradictory commands, as Bodin constructs the example, entails the possibility of anarchy. And even if contradictory commands were

A second way of mixing constitutions (as distinct from sharing) is by distributing the rights of sovereignty to different partners separately. This entails express or implied coordinating rules by which the powers thus separated, and above all the legislative power, are adjusted to each other's functions. It supposes, more specifically, that the legislature, although supreme in making rules, cannot apply them, and cannot control directly that authority which is constitutionally charged with their execution. But this possibility was also difficult to recognize at the time that Bodin wrote. In the best-known example of "mixture," the classical Roman republic, the highest forms of executive and judicial power were joined with the legislative in the people, so that in this respect it was technically not mixed. And in European monarchies, executive and legislative power were linked in the person of the king. Indeed, even Locke, much later on, who recommended the separation of executive and legislative power and had a clear example of it in the English constitution, still thought that the former was naturally subject to the latter, and that the executive independence of the English king hinged on his legislative veto. Without that veto, Locke implied, the two houses of Parliament would be entitled to make and unmake executives at will.[13]

Bodin's attempt to show that distribution of powers must be futile as a scheme of mixture, thus starts, not unexpectedly, by holding that all other powers would be in conflict with the power to make law. And as though to complicate the issue, he adds, alongside the legislative, another all-inclusive power (as Bodin interprets it), the right of taking oaths of fealty. The breakdown of the attempted distribution follows from the conflict between these two powers, without excluding resistance also arising from the independent claims of all the rest. But no matter how the picture is construed, it is evident enough that Bodin is innocent of any notion of constitutional coordination of co-equal parts:

> Someone may object, however, that it might be possible to construct a state wherein the people creates the officers, disposes of expenditures, and grants pardons – which are three prerogatives of sovereignty; where the nobility makes the laws, decides on

excluded, so that the effect of disagreement were merely to leave existing law in force, the outcome would not be democracy. The vote of one or of a few could veto the will of the many. For this last misunderstanding as it appears in Henning, Arnisaeus, and Daniel Otto, see Franklin, "Sovereignty and the Mixed Constitution," pp. 321, 327.

> peace and war, and levies duties and taxes – which are also prerogatives of sovereignty; and where there exists, in addition, a royal magistrate standing above all others to whom the people as a whole and each person in particular render fealty and homage, and who judges in the last resort without there being any means of appealing from his decision or presenting a civil request (*requeste civile*) [for a rehearing]. This, apparently, would be a way of dividing the rights and marks of sovereignty and composing a state that was aristocratic, royal, and democratic all at once. But I answer that no such state has ever existed and that none can be made or even imagined because the prerogatives of sovereignty are indivisible. For the part that has power to make law for everyone – that is, to command or forbid whatever it pleases without anyone being able to appeal from, or even oppose its commands – that part, I say, will forbid the others to make peace or war, to levy taxes, or to render fealty and homage without its leave; and he to whom fealty and liege homage is due will obligate the nobility and people to render homage to no one but himself. Hence it must always come to arms until such time as sovereignty resides in a prince, in the lesser part of the people, or in all the people (p. 103).

Bodin's idea that sovereignty is indivisible was thus based on serious confusions. Of his two claims, however, the contention that the prerogatives of sovereignty could not be separated was more or less consistent with existing evidence. For the French and other contemporary kingships, Bodin would hardly have been aware of any problem. In these systems, all authority characteristically flowed from the crown, and no decisions on high matters could be taken, at least in principle, unless the king approved. In the classical Roman republic, on the other hand, the Senate, and even certain magistrates, sometimes exercised high prerogatives of sovereignty in apparent independence of the people, whom Bodin declared to be the sovereign. But by liberal doses of the notion of tacit consent, he was able to argue, with some degree of plausibility, that such exertions of power, in so far as they were not sheer usurpations, were done on the people's behalf and by its sufferance.

But the claim that sovereignty, and most typically the power to make law, cannot be shared was much less consistent with the facts, and Bodin could maintain it for certain major systems only by misconstruing their institutional arrangements. He failed to recognize that the people in the earlier phase of the Roman republic could not act without authorization or confirmation by the Senate which thereby shared its power, and he overlooked the powers of analogous councils in other ancient and modern city-states. On the other hand, in treating contemporary European kingships, the thesis of undivided sovereignty could have seemed unproblematic to Bodin, at least at the time of the *Methodus*, because he had not yet arrived at a clear definition of the scope of sovereign power. Only thus was he able to account for French constitutional realities without acknowledging that sovereignty was shared.

For despite the centralization and growth of royal power in the Renaissance, medieval notions of limited government still lingered on in French constitutional opinion. Commentators in the main tradition, going back to Claude de Seyssel (1519), held that the king of France, although sovereign and the source of all authority, was expected to act according to the law and not to change it without the advice of some semi-independent council like the Parlement of Paris.[14] Bodin not only accepted these restraints on royal power, but gave them even greater scope and weight. He held that a king of France could not change well-established law without the consent of the provincial or general Estates, and that decrees in conflict with that law could be refused enforcement by the Parlements.[15]

The admission of these limitations seems at first sight in glaring conflict with Bodin's claim that sovereignty, undivided, was vested in the king. But when he wrote the *Methodus*, Bodin was implicitly working with a concept of limited supremacy. A king's authority, accordingly, could be sovereign yet less than absolute. He could be bound by fundamental law, in the broader sense of well-established custom, which he could not change without consent. But if his regular powers were normally sufficient for the conduct of affairs, and if nothing could be done except from his initiative, he seemed nonetheless to be supreme. By such criteria a proper monarch like the king of France could be distinguished from the doge of Venice or the emperor of Germany, who were little more than figureheads, and might even be deposed for cause.

There is a certain common sense in this relaxed conception of supremacy, and it might be roughly workable.[16] But as later writers use it, it is ultimately too flexible. The distinction between fundamental and ordinary law (which parallels the distinction between constituent and ordinary sovereignty) is legitimate, and indispensable, in constitutional theory. But where the scope of "fundamental" becomes too indefinite and broad, the utility of sovereignty as a juridical concept is undermined. Bodin would have done better, therefore, to have defined the ruler's sovereignty as absolute (except with respect to the law of nature and fundamental law more narrowly defined), and have conceded that its functions were divided among the king, the Parlements, and the Estates.

But the incoherence in Bodin's theory of sovereignty was to be eliminated in a different way. By 1576, when his *République* appeared, he had come to the conclusion that sovereignty was absolute, by which he meant that a truly sovereign authority must have all the power that a state could legitimately exercise. To this extent, the clarification of his doctrine was reasonable enough. But since Bodin continued to insist that sovereignty was indivisible, he concluded, necessarily but wrongly, that there had to exist in every commonwealth a single individual or group in which the entire power of the state was concentrated. Furthermore, since he had never doubted that the king of France was truly sovereign, it now seemed utterly clear to him that the king of France was absolute. And this applied to the kings of England and of Spain as well.

This shift to absolutism can hardly be explained by any change in Bodin's basically liberal views on the substantive issues of the time. In the second half of the *République*, where many points of public policy are discussed at length, he takes note of almost all the grievances, and embraces almost all the remedies, that were put forward in the *cahiers* of this period and that were addressed in reforming royal ordinances. Among other things, he attacks the sale of offices, the use of mercenary troops, and the custom of expensive gifts to favorites. Above all, he proposes that the burden of taxation, which he saw as a serious threat to political stability, should be gradually reduced through the repurchase and improved administration of the crown's domain.

On religious policy, Bodin's views were *politique*. The question of religious toleration was to be settled not by appealing to religious dogma, but by what best promoted political stability. Outward uniformity should be enforced wherever possible, since confessional parties were a danger to the state. But toleration should be granted wherever (as in France) a religious minority had become too strong to be repressed conveniently. These recommendations were substantially in line with the qualified and provisional toleration reluctantly proffered by the government in the truces of the civil war. It was not a generous policy, but in the circumstances of the time it was probably the most one could reasonably expect. It could, moreover, lead its proponents into opposition politics. The policy of toleration as well as other measures of reform had considerable public support, and recourse to an Estates assembly was an obvious means of pressing them upon the government.

What, then, led Bodin to revise his view of sovereignty? One element, almost surely, was further reflection on the logic of indivisibility, a thesis which had earlier been more or less intuitive. Bodin must now have reflected that if there were significant acts of governance that a king could not perform without the consent of the Estates or Parlement, then these consenting agents must have a share in his authority. Hence, consistent with the principle of indivisibility, he would have concluded that sovereignty was absolute – that the exercise of supreme authority could not be restrained within its territory by any independent agent.

But Bodin would have been confirmed in this conclusion by another, more immediately political, concern with the issue of resistance to a tyrant-king. At the time of the *Methodus* he had managed to avoid this question. Despite the existence, since the early 1560s, of a formidable Protestant party that had come into armed conflict with the government on more than one occasion, Bodin was optimistic that civil war could be avoided. He was tempted to believe that the various acts of toleration issued under Charles IX, combined with the good sense of the community, would lead to lasting peace. Ten years later, however, in the aftermath of the St. Bartholomew's Day massacre and recurrent civil war, Bodin feared for the very existence of the state. He agreed with the Huguenots that the war had been provoked by the tyrannical tactics of the crown, for which Machiavellianism could be blamed. But the right of resistance, which was publicly asserted by the Huguenots as a right against the king himself, left him thoroughly alarmed. It seemed to Bodin to be nothing less than a recipe for anarchy.[17]

Yet the key to resistance doctrine in the sixteenth century was the very set of restraints on royal power that Bodin had earlier been inclined to admit. The Huguenot resistance theorists cited these restraints as proof that the people was supreme. Fearful of risings by the general community, they looked to the Estates and higher magistrates as powers especially constituted to restrain a tyrant-king on behalf of the community, in the manner of the ancient Spartan ephors.[18] Bodin must thus have seen, at least intuitively, that binding restraints upon the ruler implied some sense in which the community was higher than the king, and that some right of resistance was inherent in its representatives. It would have seemed to follow, therefore, that the absolute power of the king of France, and of every other proper sovereign, was not only an analytic truth, but the very foundation of political stability.[19]

The outcome, accordingly, on Bodin's revised idea of sovereignty was systematic elimination, in the *République*, of all enforceable limitations on the king's authority. This is not to say that there were no moral restrictions. Bodin strenuously insisted that absolute kings were subject to the law of nature – that they were bound to respect the liberty and property of free subjects,* and that they were obligated by contracts entered into with private citizens. On this basis, Bodin even managed to hold that, except in emergencies, new taxation required the consent of the Estates if it was not to be a mere taking of the subject's property. But such restrictions could never be a ground for legitimate resistance, since for violations of the law of nature the king was answerable to God alone. In construing his obligations, furthermore, a sovereign prince did not require approval from the courts or the Estates. A prudent king, Bodin believed, would respect the remonstrations of the Parlement, and he recommended that the Estates be frequently consulted. But these were in no way binding obligations. They were mere recommendations of humanity and prudence.[20]

Bodin continued to believe that a king was also "bound" by customary fundamental law. But this domain of law, which had been

* This would not apply to lordly or despotic monarchy in the "Asiatic" style, in which the king rules like a master over slaves. Bodin admits it as legitimate, but regards it as alien to Europe which knows only "royal" monarchy, or monarchy according to law (*monarchie royale, ou légitime*): "Royal monarchy, or monarchy according to law, is one in which subjects obey the monarch's laws and the monarch obeys the laws of nature, the subjects retaining their natural liberty and the proprietorship of their goods. Lordly monarchy [*la monarchie seigneuriale*] is one in which the prince makes himself the master [*seigneur*] of properties and persons by force of arms in a just war and governs his subjects as the father of a family governs his slaves" (1961, II, 2, p. 273). The difference between the two forms of kingship, Bodin holds, does not extend to the nature of the state or sovereignty as such, but is merely a difference in the mode of governance.

left vague and broad in the *Methodus*, was now narrowed down to two arrangements: one prescribing the rule of succession to the throne; the other forbidding alienation of the royal domain without consent. Both rules were designed to keep the state intact, rather than to limit the royal right of governance. Their guarantee, moreover, was simply that attempted alterations or alienations by a sitting king would be disallowed upon his death. Hence neither the law of nature nor fundamental law could justify a challenge to absolute authority, or resistance to a sitting king.[21]

This systematic elimination of binding institutional restraints was a distortion of constitutional practice. But given the elements of ambiguity in the French tradition, the break was not easy to detect. The obligation of the king to keep existing law had always been presented tactfully. In the 1560s, the obtaining of consent before changing well-established law was considered to be the normal and unvarying practice, but the invocation of absolute authority had not been totally excluded. The right of the Estates had not been specified precisely in the older commentators, and there was even some uncertainty attaching to the status of the Parlements.[22] The Parlements did not assert a veto on royal legislation, so much as a right of continued remonstration until such time as their complaints were heeded. Hence the change in Bodin's view of sovereignty in 1576 would not have been obvious to many of his readers, and Bodin himself must have regarded his position in the *République* as a mere clarification of a doctrine he had always held.

As Bodin presented it, moreover, the idea of absolute kingship would not have seemed threatening to moderate contemporaries. In one way or another he managed to account for almost all the limitations that had been traditionally considered indispensable. Accused by a Genevan critic of having favored despotism, Bodin replied with indignation:

> I am amazed by those who believe that I have given more power to one man than is becoming to an honest citizen. For specifically in Book I, chapter 8 of my *République*, and in other passages as well, I was the very first, even in these dangerous times, unhesitatingly to refute the opinions of those who would expand the right of the treasury and the regalian prerogatives, on the grounds that they give kings unlimited power beyond the laws of God and nature. And what could be more public-spirited

> [*populare*] than what I have dared to write – that even kings are not allowed to levy taxes without the fullest consent of the citizens? Of what importance is it that I have also held that princes are more strictly bound by divine and natural law than those who are subject to their rule? Or that they are obligated by their contracts like any other citizen? Yet almost all the masters of juristic science have taught the opposite.[23]

These limitations are no longer anchored in binding customary law, and Bodin had thereby undermined the legal force of checks upon the king. But he still expected them to operate as in the past. He confidently believed that the complaints and administrative pressures of the magistrates would restrain impulsive rulers, and he optimistically expected that the political value of the Estates was sufficient to assure their consultation. Bodin's account of sovereignty would thus have appeared to be compatible with civilized and law-abiding government. Yet it seemed to provide an ironclad defense against any justification of resistance from below, which was to recommend it strongly in the troubled circumstances of the later sixteenth century.

Principal events in Bodin's life

1529/30	Born, Angers.
1545	Enters the Carmelite order.
1545–47	Resides at Carmelite house in Paris; pursues humanist studies at the royal Collège de quatres langues.
1547	Charged with heresy.
1548–49	Obtains release from his vows on the plea that he had professed them at too early an age.
1550s	Studies law at the University of Toulouse where he held a minor teaching position. Fails to secure a regular academic post.
1560–61	Barrister in the Parlement of Paris.
1562	Outbreak of the French religious wars which continue, with interruptions, until 1598.
1566	Publishes his *Methodus ad facilem historiarum cognitionem.*
1570	Appointed royal commissioner for the Forest of Normandy.
1571	Appointed master of requests and counsellor to Francis, duke of Alençon, the youngest brother of King Charles IX and next in line to the throne upon the accession of Henry III (1574).
1572	Massacre of St. Bartholomew.
1576	Publishes *Les six livres de la république.*
	Attends the Estates-General at Blois (1576–77) as a deputy for the Third Estate of Vermandois.
1581	Visits England in the entourage of Alençon, a suitor of Elizabeth I.

1582	Alençon's misadventure in Antwerp.
1584	Alençon dies.
1586	Latin translation of *Les six livres de la république* (*De republica libri sex*) done by Bodin himself.
1587	Becomes royal attorney in the presidial court of Laon.
1588–89	Assassination of both the duke and the cardinal of Guise, leaders of the Catholic League (December 1588), at instigation of Henry III; assassination of Henry III (July 1589); contestation by Catholic party of Henry of Navarre's claim to be recognized as Henry IV – lead to the final phase of the religious wars.
1588–94	Catholic League controls Laon. Bodin collaborates.
1588–94	Composition at Laon of works on ethics, natural philosophy, and religion, some published only posthumously. Completes the *Colloquium heptaplomeres* in 1593.
1596	Bodin dies.

Bibliography

Bodin's works (not including letters and translations)

The date of the first edition is given in the left-hand margin; the date of composition (in bold type) is also given in the margin where there is a significant disparity with the date of the first published edition; an English translation, where available, is given in brackets. For Latin works not translated into English, translations into French are mentioned. An extended bibliography containing all known editions of each work and editions of Bodin's letters may be found in Horst Denzer (ed.), *Jean Bodin, Verhandlungen der internationalen Bodin Tagung in München* (Munich, 1973), pp. 492–500. But facsimile reprints and new editions continue to appear.

1559 *Oratio de instituenda in republica in juventute ad Senatum Populumque Tolosatem*, in Pierre Mesnard (ed.), *Œuvres philosophiques de Jean Bodin* (Paris, 1951), pp. 7–30 [*Address to the Senate and people of Toulouse on Education of Youth in the Commonwealth*, trans. George Albert Moore (Chevy Chase, 1965)].

1566 *Methodus ad facilem historiarum cognitionem*, in Mesnard (ed.), *Œuvres philosophiques de Jean Bodin*, pp. 107–269 [*Method for the Easy Comprehension of History*, trans. Beatrice Reynolds (New York, 1945)].

1568 *La vie chère au XVIe siècle. La response de Jean Bodin à M. de Malestroit*, ed. Henri Hauser (Paris, 1932) [*The Response of Jean Bodin to the Paradoxes of M. Malestroit*, edition of 1578, trans. George Albert Moore (Chevy Chase, 1946–47)].

1576 *Les six livres de la république* (Paris, 1583; reprinted Aalen, 1961). Another edition, based on text of 1593 (Paris, 1986) [*The Six Bookes of a Commonweale*, trans. Richard Knolles (London, 1606), reprinted with apparatus by Kenneth D. McRae (Cambridge, Mass., 1962). *I sei libri dello Stato de Jean Bodin*, trans. and ed. Margherita Isnardi Parente, 2 vols. containing Books I–IV (Turin, 1988). Abbreviated IP.]

1577 *Recueil de tout ce qui s'est negotié en la compagnie du Tiers Estat de France en l'assemblée générale des trois estats, assignez par le roy en la villed de Blois, au novembre 1576* (n.p., 1577).

1578 *Juris universi distributio*, in Mesnard (ed.), *Œuvres*
c.1560 *philosophiques de Jean Bodin*, pp. 71–80 [*Tableau du droit universel*, *ibid.*, pp. 83–97]. Another edition, Latin and French (Paris, 1985).

1580 *De la démonomanie des sorciers* (Paris, 1580; reprinted Paris, 1979; Hildesheim, 1988).

1581 *Apologie de René Herpin pour la République de J. Bodin*, an answer to critics written by Bodin himself; included as an appendix in *Six livres de la république* (1583; reprinted 1961, 1986).

1586 *De republica libri sex* (Latin version of *République*), (Paris, 1586).

1588 *Sapientiae moralis epitome ... ab Helia Bodino Joannis filio collecta*, in Paul Lawrence Rose (ed.), *Jean Bodin, Selected Writings on Philosophy, Religion, and Politics* (Geneva, 1980), pp. 21–31. The text is by Bodin himself and comes with a parallel translation into French.

1596 *Universae naturae theatrum* (Lyon and Paris, 1596) [*Le théâtre de la nature universelle ...*, trans. Fr. de Fougerolles (Lyon, 1597)].

1596 *Paradoxon, quod nec virtus ulla in mediocritate, nec summum hominis bonum in virtutis actione consistere possit* (Paris, 1596) [*Le Paradoxe de J. Bodin ... qu'il n'y a pas une seule vertu en médiocrité, ny au milieu de deux vices ...*, Bodin's own translation published posthumously (Paris, 1598; reprinted in Paul Lawrence Rose [ed.], *Selected Writings on Philosophy, Religion, and Politics*, pp. 43–75)].

1857 *Colloquium heptaplomeres de rerum sublimium arcanis abditis*,
1593 ed. L. Noack (first complete edition, Schwerin, 1857;

reprinted Hildesheim, New York, 1970) [*Colloquium of the Seven about Secrets of the Sublime*, trans. Marion Leathers Daniels Kuntz (Princeton, 1975)].

Recent translations of the *Six livres de la république*

Isnardi Parente, Margherita (ed. and trans.), *I sei libri dello Stato di Jean Bodin*, 2 vols. containing Books I–IV (Turin, 1988). Abbreviated IP in the text.

Wimmer, Bernd (trans.), *Jean Bodin, Sechs Bücher über den Staat*, ed. P.C. Mayer-Tasch, 2 vols., I (Munich, 1981), II (Munich, 1986).

Other works

This is a selective list concentrating on books and articles dealing with Bodin's theory of sovereignty and its background. A comprehensive bibliography as of 1973, compiled by Horst Denzer, may be found in Denzer (ed.), *Verhandlungen der internationalen Bodin Tagung in München* (Munich 1973), and an extensive bibliography as of 1989 in Simone Goyard-Fabre, *Jean Bodin et le droit de la république* (Paris, 1989). The conference proceedings referred to below are *Verhandlungen in München* (Munich, 1973); *La "République" di Jean Bodin: Atti del convegno di Perugia. 14–15 Novembre 1980* (Florence, 1981); *Jean Bodin, Actes du Colloque Interdisciplinaire d'Angers 24–27 Mai, 1984* (Angers, 1985).

Brown, John L., *The Methodus ad facilem historiarum cognitionem, A Critical Study* (Washington, DC, 1939).

Caprariis, Vittorio de, *Propaganda e pensiero politico durante le guerre di religione, I, 1559–1572* (Naples, 1959).

Chauviré, Roger, *Jean Bodin, auteur de la République* (La Flèche, 1914).

Church, William F., *Constitutional Thought in Sixteenth-Century France* (Cambridge, Mass., 1941; reprinted, New York, 1969).

Comparato, Vittor Ivo, "Sulla teoria della funzione pubblica nella *République* de Jean Bodin," *Atti di Perugia* (Florence, 1981), pp. 93–112.

Franklin, Julian H., *Jean Bodin and the Sixteenth-Century Revolution in the Methodology of Law and History* (New York, 1963).

Constitutionalism and Resistance in the Sixteenth Century (New York, 1969).

Jean Bodin and the Rise of Absolutist Theory (Cambridge, 1973).

"Jean Bodin and the End of Medieval Constitutionalism," *Verhandlungen in München* (Munich, 1973), pp. 151–66.

"Sovereignty and the Mixed Constitution: Bodin and his Critics," in J.H. Burns (ed.), *The Cambridge History of Political Thought 1450–1700* (Cambridge, 1991).

Garosci, Aldo, *Jean Bodin: politica e diritto nel Rinascimento francese* (Milan, 1934).

Gierke, Otto van, *The Development of Political Theory*, trans. H. Fertig (New York, 1966).

Giesey, Ralph E., "Medieval Jurisprudence in Bodin's Concept of Sovereignty," *Verhandlungen in München* (Munich, 1973), pp. 167–86.

Goyard-Fabre, Simone, *Jean Bodin et le droit de la république* (Paris, 1989).

Hancke, E., *Bodin, eine Studie über der Begriff der Souveränität* (Breslau, 1894; reprinted Aalen, 1969).

Hinrichs, Ernst, "Das Furstenbild Bodins and die Krise der französische Renaissancemonarchie," *Verhandlungen in München* (Munich, 1973), pp. 261–80.

Isnardi Parente, Margherita, "Jean Bodin su Tirannide e Signoria nella *République*," *Atti di Perugia* (Florence, 1981), pp. 61–78.

"Les *Metēbolai Politeion* revisits: Bodin, *La République*, IV," *Actes d'Angers* (Angers, 1985), pp. 49–52.

"Introduzione," *I sei libri dello Stato di Jean Bodin* (Turin, 1988).

Kelley, Donald R., *Foundations of Modern Historical Scholarship: Language, Law, and History in the French Renaissance* (New York and London, 1970).

"The Development and Context of Bodin's Method," *Verhandlungen in München* (Munich, 1973), pp. 123–50.

Marocco Stuardi, Donatella, "La teoria della giustizia armonica nella *République*," *Atti di Perugia* (Florence, 1981), pp. 134–44.

Marongiu, Antonio, "Bodin, lo Stato e gli stati," *Atti di Perugia* (Florence, 1981), pp. 78–92.

"Bodin et le consentement à l'impôt," *Actes d'Angers* (Angers, 1985), pp. 365–74.

McRae, Kenneth D., "Introduction," *Jean Bodin, Six Bookes of a Commonweale* (Cambridge, Mass., 1962).

"Bodin and the Development of Empirical Political Science," *Verhandlungen in München* (Munich 1973), pp. 333–42.

Mesnard, Pierre, *L'Essor de la philosophie politique au XVIe siècle* (2nd ed., Paris, 1951), pp. 71–121.

Moreau-Reibel, Jean, *Jean Bodin et le droit public comparé dans ses rapports avec la philosophie de l'histoire* (Paris, 1933).

Olivier-Martin, F., *Histoire du droit français* (Paris, 1948).

Salmon, J.H.M., "Bodin and the Monarchomachs," *Verhandlungen in München* (Munich, 1973), pp. 343–58.

Skinner, Quentin, *The Foundations of Modern Political Thought*, 2 vols. (Cambridge, 1978), II, 3.

Villey, Michel, "La Justice harmonique selon Bodin," *Verhandlungen in München* (Munich, 1973), pp. 69–86.

Wolfe, Martin, "Jean Bodin on Taxes: The Sovereignty–Taxes Paradox," *Political Science Quarterly*, 83 (2), June 1968, pp. 268–84.

Works, other than those mentioned above, those cited in editor's notes or in the introductory apparatus

Alciato, Andrea, "Paradoxa," in *Opera*, IV (Basel, 1582).

Arnisaeus, Henning, "Doctrina politica," in *Opera politica omnia* (Strasbourg, 1648).

Baxter, Christopher R., "Jean Bodin's Daemon and his Conversion to Judaism," *Verhandlungen in München* (Munich, 1973), pp. 1–21.

Besold, Christoph, "De majestate in genere ejusque juribus specialibus . . . accedit tractatio singularis de reipublicae statu mixto," in *Operis politici, editio nova* (Strasbourg, 1626).

Du Haillan, Bernard de Girard, *De l'estat et succez des affaires de France* (Paris, 1571).

Du Tillet, Jean, *Les mémoires et recherches* (Rouen, 1577).

Giesey, Ralph E., *If Not, Not: The Oath of the Aragonese and the Legendary Laws of Sobrarbre* (Princeton, 1968).

Gilmore, Myron P., *Argument from Roman Law in Political Thought: 1200–1600* (Cambridge, Mass., 1941).

Locke, John, *Two Treatises of Government*, ed. Peter Laslett (Cambridge, 1988).

Rose, Paul L., *Bodin and the Great God of Nature, the Moral and Religious Universe of a Judaizer* (Geneva, 1980).

Seyssell, Claude de, *The Monarchy of France*, trans. J.H. Hexter, ed. Donald R. Kelley (New Haven and London, 1981).

Note on the text

Bodin's *République* was translated into English in 1606 by Richard Knolles, and that translation has been reprinted (1962) under the editorship of Kenneth D. McRae with an extremely valuable introduction, scholarly apparatus, and index. The only other rendition of the *République* in English is a highly condensed abridgement by M.J. Tooley (New York, 1955). Neither version seemed useful for the present purpose. The Tooley condensation is too brief and too selective; the Knolles translation is archaic in style, language, and orthography and, as I shall explain below, it uses Bodin's texts in a way that no longer measures up to scholarly standards. I thus decided to embark upon a wholly new translation.

My choice of texts, however, requires further explanation. The *République* comes down to us in two principal versions: one stemming from the original French edition of 1576; the other going back to the Latin translation, done by Bodin himself, which appeared in 1586. The French version went through at least seventeen editions in Bodin's lifetime. Many of these, as Kenneth D. McRae points out, are mere reprints of earlier editions with minor changes not necessarily authorized by Bodin himself. But in the folio editions of 1577 and 1578, Bodin undertook major revisions, which were then incorporated into the octavo editions that began in 1579. Among these the earlier revisions are the best. After about 1580, McRae observes, "the principal change in the French text is a gradual deterioration due to the cumulation of misprints."[1] In 1961, one of the better French versions, the octavo edition of Jacques du Puys (Paris, 1583) was reprinted in facsimile by the Scientia Press of

Aalen, Germany, and has become the predominant one. It is the text that scholars commonly cite, and has been taken as the master text for translations into German and Italian.

One last revision of the *République*, however, was still to come with Bodin's Latin translation of 1586. It is a very free translation in which the French text is largely rewritten, and as he reworked the text, Bodin strengthened it in many ways. In the four chapters rendered in this present volume, there are several important alterations of his basic view of sovereignty. New historical illustrations are sometimes added, and old ones are often corrected on points of detail. Passages in the French that were obscure or ambiguous for lack of careful editing are regularly cleared up in the process of rewriting. These gains, to be sure, are partly offset by corresponding losses. The translation evinces a certain impatience and offhandedness that sometimes seem to make things worse. The Latin text often becomes too abstract, as useful details and explanations in the French are left aside in the process of rewriting. Yet at other times the new version is self-indulgently expansive, as though Bodin was unable to curb his well-known proclivity for rambling digressions and irrelevant detail. His negligence as an editor, furthermore – which had caused difficulties in the French in the process of rewriting – sometimes leads to fresh obscurities in the Latin. Finally, Bodin's Latin style tends to be wordy and overblown. Although it is not likely that anyone will ever claim literary distinction for Bodin's writing, there is often a salty freshness in the French that gets lost in the translation. Even so, the Latin version is distinctly superior and, all things being equal, should be taken as the master text for an English translation.

Circumstances, however, pointed to a different course. A translation, to be useful, ought to be based on a version of the original that scholars regularly use and cite, unless there are very strong considerations to the contrary. The considerations in favor of Bodin's Latin text, however, are not decisive. Indeed, a translation from the French with copious variations from the Latin would be almost as good, and in some ways better, than the other way around.* And at a time when

* A third possibility would be to conflate the two versions, the technique used by Richard Knolles in his English translation of 1606. Although more often favoring the French, Knolles took now the French and now the Latin as the master text as he deemed best for any given topic, often interweaving juicy phrases or informative details from the other. Yet translation from one text with variations from the other gives much the same result, with far less risk of the translator substituting his own sense of how the text should read

Latin is no longer required even for serious humanists unless their specialty demands it, the French version, especially the Paris edition of 1583, has clear priority.

This edition of 1583, furthermore, is the master text for Margherita Isnardi Parente's translation into Italian, the first four books of which have now been published in two volumes. This translation is of very great importance because of the scholarly apparatus that accompanies it. All versions of the *République* present a huge number of citations in the margins* which are often difficult to decipher. This is especially true of the many citations to Roman civil law and to its commentators, which are especially numerous in the chapters translated here, and are given in an obsolete medieval form. Professor Isnardi Parente has not only undertaken to decipher and modernize all of Bodin's citations; she has also checked them for accuracy, suggested correct citations where Bodin's appear to be incorrect or obscure, and offered corrected readings where Bodin has quoted sources inaccurately. Beyond this, she has attempted to supply sources and corrected versions of quotations, paraphrases, and allusions that appear in the text without reference or with the reference only vaguely suggested.† A translation of Bodin into English, therefore, should allow the reader to profit from Isnardi Parente's impressive contribution, and is best done by working from the same master text, the French edition of 1583. Bernd Wimmer has already adopted that solution for the translation into German, and I have done so here as well. Like Wimmer, I have not carried over Isnardi Parente's apparatus,‡ but have simply referred the interested reader to her text (abbreviated IP). Responsible transfer of her results to an English translation even of the French, would be a labor of many years, let

for Bodin's. Although Knolles' judgment is generally excellent and his weaving artful, he sometimes seems, at least to me, to make the wrong choice of master text and to alter the emphasis of Bodin's words by interweaving. I even suspect that, on occasions, the reason for his choice of texts was merely to avoid a passage difficult to translate in the other. The conflation of texts, in any event, is yet another reason why Knolles' work is obsolete.

* Ralph E. Giesey (*Medieval Jurisprudence*, pp. 167–8) has counted 600 separate marginal citations to Roman civil and canon law in Book I, chapters 8 and 10 alone, and estimates about 6,000 such citations in the work as a whole.

† Dr. Albert Cremer of the Max-Planck-Institut für Geschichte in Göttingen has been working on a comprehensive comparison of all the texts of the *République*, which may some day prepare the way for a full-scale critical edition.

‡ I have, however, generally followed her determinations as to when Bodin, apparently quoting, is really paraphrasing. I have simply used or not used quotation marks accordingly.

alone a translation of the Latin where the marginalia are often changed. Given present needs, this probably does not make sense for any translation from the French, and surely not for one directed to the general reader.

The present translation is therefore based on the French edition of 1583 as reprinted in 1961. Bodin's marginalia have been left out except in a few instances where they seem to be of special interest to the general student.* I have attempted to include all variations authored by Bodin himself that seem to improve or enlarge his argument. Two or three of these, suggested by McRae or Isnardi Parente, are from earlier French editions. All the rest are from the Latin edition of 1586, in the quotation of which I have preferred to err on the side of generosity. I have tried to include not only every change of doctrine in the Latin, but also all new details and corrections of detail which appear to strengthen Bodin's account of the institutions or political history of systems like the Roman or the French that were especially important for him and his contemporaries. I have also tried to include all improvements of meaning where the French is in any way ambiguous or obscure. It is only where the change in the Latin seems trivial, exotic, digressive, or merely rhetorical, that I have simply passed it over. I have also indicated, although more cautiously, omissions from the French that seem to be deliberate and significant corrections.

*Topic headings that appear irregularly in the margins are probably by a printer rather than Bodin and have been omitted.

Notes on format

1 The endnotes are used for comments on and explanations of the text.

2 The footnotes are used mainly for variations from other texts, for the English translation of quotations (mostly Latin) that Bodin gives in the original language, and for Bodin's own notes (in the few instances where these are included). Where the notes are from Bodin, they are marked as such. Where a variation is given in a footnote and a comment seems appropriate, the latter is included in the same note. Where a quotation in some other language is accompanied by Bodin's own translation into French, an English translation is given in the text rather than Bodin's French translation.

3 Parentheses are used not only to give a word or phrase from the French original, as is standard practice, but on occasion the Latin original along with it. Square brackets are used to supply an appositive word of explanation not included in the French. Special brackets { } are used where the appositive word or phrase is confirmed by the Latin text or directly taken from it.

4 Obvious typographical errors in the text are corrected without indication. Minor details appearing in Bodin's notes, such as the proper name of a king or the date of a treaty, are simply transferred to the text in square brackets. Where similar transfers of detail are from the Latin, they are indicated by special brackets { }.

5 Page references to the Latin text include line references from the original edition, such as B10, D6 and so on. The top line of each page in the Latin is indicated as though it were A1.

6 Page numbers corresponding to the French text of 1583 are placed directly in the text, using square brackets and boldface type, for example, **[211]**. Page numbers corresponding to the Italian translation are placed in the margins, using special brackets and italics, for example, {*454*}.

Notes on translation

1 Where there is doubt as to whether Bodin intended to quote or to paraphrase, I have generally followed Isnardi Parente's indications. But I have not reported or duplicated her efforts to supply corrected versions and citations.

2 Dates in Bodin's texts have not been corrected for calendar changes, and equivalents for old French monetary units have not been supplied.

3 The term *estat*, as distinguished from *république*, technically refers to the system of sovereign power and not to the organized political community over which the sovereign rules. Hence the two terms are normally translated as "state" and "commonwealth" respectively. But Bodin sometimes uses *république* to mean a current system of power, in which case I have rendered it as "state." On very rare occasions, he uses the word to designate a community in which the sovereign is a collective body rather than an individual, in which case I have translated it as "republic." On one occasion, where the emphasis of *estat* is on the constitutional pattern, I have translated it as "regime." Bodin often uses *estat populaire* for democracy, and *seigneurie*, *seigneurie aristocratique*, or *estat aristocratique* for aristocracy. I have always used "democracy" or "aristocracy," and have tried to convey in other ways the differences of tone that Bodin sometimes creates by his choice of terms. Thus in some cases, but not at all consistently, *démocratie* seems intended to convey something more plebeian than *estat populaire*.

The term *estat* can also mean either a social class or a representative body based on classes. When referring to the former, I have rendered it as "estates"; when referring to the latter, as "Estates."

République, edition of 1583 (Paris), table of contents

Book I

Book II

Book III

Book IV

Book V

Book VI

BOOK I, CHAPTER 8
On sovereignty[1]

345} Sovereignty is the absolute and perpetual power* of a commonwealth, which the Latins call *maiestas*; the Greeks *akra exousia*, *kurion arche*, and *kurion politeuma*; and the Italians *segnioria*, a word they use for private persons as well as for those who have full control of the state, while the Hebrews call it *tomech shévet* – that is, the highest power of command.† We must now formulate a definition of sovereignty because no jurist or political philosopher has defined it, even though it is the chief point, and the one that needs most to be explained, in a treatise on the commonwealth. Inasmuch as we have said that a commonwealth is a just government, with sovereign power, of several households and of that which they have in common,‡ we need to clarify the meaning of sovereign power.

I have said that this power is perpetual, because it can happen that one or more people have absolute power given to them for some certain period of time, upon the expiration of which they are no more

*L78, D6 substitutes, "Sovereignty is supreme and absolute power over citizens and subjects" (*Maiestas est summa in cives ac subditos legibusque soluta potestas*). The Latin thus speaks of "supreme and absolute" without reference to "perpetual." But "perpetual" is effectively added to the definition just a few lines further on at 79, A5.

The distinction between citizen and subject that appears in the Latin is spelled out in chapter 6. A citizen is distinguished from a slave by personal freedom, and from an alien by the right to enjoy common privileges. But citizenship does not necessarily imply political participation as in Aristotle. "Speaking properly . . . [a citizen] is nothing other than a free subject holding by another's sovereignty" (1961, p. 68).

†L78, D11 adds, "Sovereignty (*maiestas*), says Festus, is taken from greatness (*magnitudo*)."

‡"A commonwealth is . . . have in common" repeats, with slight variations, the celebrated definition with which the *République* opens, *République est un droit gouvernment de plusieurs familles, et ce qui leur est commun, avec puissance souveraine.*

than private subjects. And even while they are in power, they cannot call themselves sovereign princes.[2] They are but trustees and custodians of that power until such time as it pleases the people or the prince to take it back, for the latter always remains in lawful possession (*qui en demeure tousiours saisi*). For just as those who lend someone else their goods always remain its owners and possessors, so also those who give power and authority to judge or to command, either for some limited and definite period of time or for as much and as long a time as it shall please them. They still remain lawfully pos-
{346} sessed of power and jurisdiction, which the others exercise in the manner of a loan or grant on sufferance (*précaire*). That is why the [Roman civil] law[3] holds that the governor of a region, or the lieutenant of a prince, being a trustee and guardian of someone else's power, returns it when his term has expired. And in this respect, it makes no difference whether the officer is high or petty.

If it were otherwise [123], and the absolute power conceded to a lieutenant of the prince were called sovereignty, he would be able to use it against his prince, who would then be no more than a cipher, and the subject would then command his lord, and the servant his master, which would be absurd. The person of the sovereign, according to the law, is always excepted no matter how much power and authority he grants to someone else; and he never gives so much that he does not hold back even more. He is never prevented from commanding, or from assuming cognizance – by substitution, concurrence, removal, or any way he pleases – of any cause that he left to the jurisdiction of a subject. Nor does it matter whether the subject is a commissioner or an officer.[4] In either case the sovereign can take away the power with which he was endowed by virtue of the commission or the statute of his office, or he can retain him on sufferance in so far and for as long as it pleases him.

{347} Having laid down these maxims as the foundations of sovereignty, we may conclude that neither the Roman dictator, nor the Spartan harmoste, nor the aesymnetes at Salonica, nor he whom they call the archus in Malta, nor the balia of old in Florence – all of whom had the same duties – nor the regents in kingdoms, nor any other commissioner or magistrate who had absolute power for a limited time to dispose of the affairs of the commonwealth, had sovereignty. This holds even though the early dictators had full power and had it in the best possible form, or *optima lege* as the ancient Latins called it. For

there was no appeal [from a dictator] in those days, and all the other officers were suspended. This was the arrangement up until the time the tribunes were established, who continued in their functions and retained their right of intercession notwithstanding the creation of a dictator. If an appeal was taken from the dictator, the tribunes assembled the commons and summoned the [complaining] parties to present the grounds of their appeal, and the dictator to defend his judgment. This is what was done when the dictator Papirius Cursor wanted to have Fabius Maximus I, the master of the horse {*magister equitum*}, put to death, and when the dictator Fabius Maximus II wanted to do the same to his master of the horse, Minutius. It thus
48} appears that the dictator was neither a prince nor a sovereign magistrate, as many have written, and that he held nothing more than a simple commission to conduct a war, or to put down sedition **[124]**, or to reform the state, or to bring in new magistrates.*

Sovereignty, then, is not limited either in power, or in function, or in length of time. As for the ten commissioners established [at Rome] for reforming customs and ordinances {*Decemviri legum ferendarum*},[5] even though they had absolute power without appeal and all the magistrates were suspended for the term of their commission, they still did not have sovereignty. For when their mission was accomplished, their power expired, in exactly the same manner as the dictator's. Thus Cincinnatus, after defeating the enemy, laid down the dictatorship, which he had held for only fifteen days; Servilius Priscus did the same after eight days; Mamercus after one. The dictator, furthermore, was [simply] named by one of the more eminent {patrician} senators {the *interrex*} and not by an edict, law, or ordinance which, in ancient times as much as now, was required for erecting an office,† as we shall explain in due course. If anyone objects that Sulla

*L80, A3 adds, "or for driving in a nail [that is, ritually marking the passage of a year]."

†L80, B2–7 corrects "The dictator, furthermore . . . erecting an office," and also adds a marginal note on the rank ordering of Roman senators, "A dictator was not named by the Senate, or the people, or the magistrates; or by a consultation of the people; or by any laws – which were always necessary for the creation of magistrates – but rather by an *interrex* who could only be of patrician blood since it was not sufficient to be an ennobled senator in order to name a dictator."

The marginal note to this passage reads, "A new man (*novus*) was someone who was the first [of his family] to obtain the honor [of high office] in the commonwealth; an ennobled man (*nobilis*) was the son of a new man; a patrician (*patricius*) was someone descended from the patriarchs and those who were enrolled by Romulus (*a patribus et conscriptis a Romulo*)."

obtained a dictatorship for eighty years by the *lex Valeria*,[6] I will answer, as Cicero did, that it was not a proper law, and not a dictatorship, but a cruel tyranny, which, in any event, he gave up four years later when the civil wars had quieted down. Moreover, Sulla allowed the tribunes to use their veto[7] freely. And although Caesar took a dictatorship for life, he too did not remove the tribunes' right of veto. But since the dictatorship had been expressly abolished by law,[8] and he had used it nevertheless as a cover for seizing the state, he was killed.

{*349*} But let us suppose that a people chooses one or several citizens, to whom it gives absolute power to manage the state and to govern freely, without having to submit to vetoes or appeals of any sort, and that this measure is reenacted every year. Shall we not say that they have sovereignty? For he is absolutely sovereign who recognizes nothing, after God, that is greater than himself. I say, however, that they do not have sovereignty, since they are nothing but trustees of a power that was confided to them for a definite period of time. Hence the people did not divest itself of sovereignty when it established one or more lieutenants with absolute power for a definite time, even though that is more generous than if the power was subject to recall at the people's pleasure without a pre-established time limit. In either case the lieutenant has nothing of his own and remains [125] answerable for his charge to the person of whom he holds the power to command, unlike a sovereign prince who is answerable only to God.

But what would we say if absolute power were conceded for nine or ten years, as it was in the early days of Athens when the people made one of the citizens sovereign and called him archon? I still maintain that he was not a prince and did not have sovereignty, but was rather a sovereign magistrate who was accountable to the people for his actions after his time in office had expired. One might still object that absolute power can be given to a citizen as I have indicated, yet without requiring him to answer to the people. Thus the Cnidians annually chose sixty citizens whom they called "amnemones" – that is to say, beyond reproach – and granted them sovereign power with no appeal from them, either during their term in office or after it, for
{*350*} anything that they had done. Yet I say that they did not have sovereignty in view of the fact that, as custodians, they were obliged to give it back when their year was up. Sovereignty thus remained in the people, and only its exercise was in the amnemones, whom one could

call sovereign magistrates, but not sovereigns pure and simple. For the first is a prince, the other is a subject; the first is a lord, the other is a servant; the first is a proprietor and in lawful possession of the sovereignty (*et saisi de la souveraineté*), the other is neither its owner nor possessor, but merely holds in trust.

The same applies to regents established during the absence or minority of sovereign princes, no matter whether edicts, orders, and letters patent are signed and sealed with the regents' signature and seal and are issued in their name, which was the practice in this kingdom prior to the ordinance of King Charles V of France, or whether it is all done in the king's name and orders are sealed with his seal. For in either case it is quite clear that, according to the law, the master is taken to have done whatever a deputy (*procureur*) did on his authority. But the regent is properly the deputy of the king and the kingdom, so that the good Count Thibaut called himself *procurator regni Francorum* (deputy of the French kingdom). Hence when the prince, either present or absent, gives absolute power to a regent or perhaps to the senate, to govern in his name, it is always the king who speaks and who commands even if the title of regent is used on edicts and letters of **[126]** command.

Thus we see that in the absence of the king of Spain, the senate of Milan and of Naples had absolute power and issued all of its com-
51} mands in its own name, as is evident from the ordinance of Emperor Charles V:

> *Senatus Mediolansensis potestatem habeat constitutiones Principis confirmandi, infirmandi, tollendi, dispensandi contra statuta, habilitationes, praerogationes, restitutiones faciendi, etc. a Senatu ne provocari possit etc., et quicquid faciet parem vim habeat, ut si a principe factum, ac decretum esset: non tamen possit delictorum gratium, ac veniam tribuere, aut literas salvi conductus reis criminum dare.**

This all but unlimited power was not given to the senate of Milan and of Naples to diminish the sovereignty of the king of Spain in any way, but rather to relieve him of bother and concern, to which must

*The senate of Milan shall have the power of confirming, invalidating, and repealing ordinances of the prince; of granting dispensations from the statutes; and of granting permissions, prerogatives, and restitutions etc.; no appeal shall lie from the Senate etc., and whatever it shall do shall have the same force as if it had been done or decreed by the prince: but it shall not grant pardon or forgiveness for crimes, or give letters of safe conduct to persons accused of criminal offenses.

also be added the fact that it was revocable at the good pleasure of him who granted it.

But let us suppose that this power is given to a lieutenant of the king for life. Is this not sovereign and perpetual power? For if perpetual were taken to mean that which never ends, sovereignty would not exist except in aristocracies and democracies, which never die. Even if the word perpetual, as used of a monarch, was understood to include not only him but his heirs, there would still be few sovereign monarchs inasmuch as there are very few that are hereditary. Those especially would not be sovereign who come to the throne by election.[9] We must, therefore, understand the word "perpetual" to mean "for the life of him who has the power."

I would add that if a sovereign magistrate, whose term is only annual or is for a fixed and limited time, contrives to prolong the power entrusted to him, it must either be by tacit consent (*de gré à gré*) or by force.[10] If by force, it is called a tyranny. Yet the tyrant is nonetheless a sovereign, just as the violent possession of a robber is true and natural possession even if against the law, and those who had it previously are dispossessed (*en sont dessaisis*).[11] But if a magistrate prolongs sovereign power by tacit consent, I say that he is not a sovereign prince, since he has nothing except by sufferance, and all the less so if no time limit is set, for then he has only a precarious
{*352*} commission (*commission précaire*).[12]

[127] It is well known that there never was a greater power than that which was given to Henry of France, duke of Anjou,[13] by King Charles IX, for it was sovereign power, and did not omit a single item of regalian prerogative.[14] Yet no one can tell me that he was a sovereign, for even if the grant had been perpetual, he was styled the king's lieutenant-general. Furthermore, the clause "So long as it shall please us (*Tant qu'il nous plaira*)" was affixed to his letters [patent] which indicates a grant on sufferance, and his power was always suspended in the king's presence.

What shall we say then of someone who has absolute power from the people for as long as he shall live? Here one must distinguish. If the absolute power is given to him pure and simple without the style of a magistrate or commissioner, and not in the form of a grant on sufferance (*précaire*), then he surely is, and has a right to call himself, a sovereign monarch. For the people has here dispossessed and stripped itself of its sovereign power in order to put him in possession of it

and to vest it in him. It has transferred all of its power, authority, prerogatives, and sovereign rights to him and [placed them] in him, in the same way as someone who has given up the possession of, and property in, something that belonged to him.* As the law says, *Ei et in eum omnem potestatem contulit.*† But if the people concedes its power to someone for as long as he shall live in the capacity of officer or lieutenant, or only to relieve itself of the exercise of its power, then he is not a sovereign, but a simple officer, lieutenant, regent, governor, or guardian and trustee of another's power. For it is the same as with a magistrate who appoints a permanent deputy and takes no active role in his jurisdiction, but leaves its entire exercise to the deputy. The
53} power of commanding and judging, and the action and the force of the law,[15] do not lie in the person of the deputy, and if he goes beyond the power given him, his acts are of no effect unless they are ratified, accepted, and approved by the person who gave him power.‡ This is the reason why King John [II of France], on his return from England, solemnly ratified the acts of Charles, his oldest son, who had been named regent, in order thereby to validate and confirm them in so far as that was needed.

So whether it is by commission, nomination to office, or delegation that one exercises someone else's power, and whether it is for a definite time or in perpetuity, he who exercises **[128]** this power is not sovereign even if he is not described as an agent or lieutenant in his letters patent. This applies even if the power is conferred by the law of the land, which is an even stronger basis than appointment (*election*). The ancient law of Scotland thus gave the entire government of the kingdom to the closest relative of a king who was in tutelage or under age {below twenty-five}, with the requirement that all business be carried on in the king's name. But the rule was suppressed because of the inconveniences that went with it.

We now turn to the other part of our definition and to what is meant by the words "absolute power." For the people or the aristocracy (*seigneurs*) of a commonwealth can purely and simply give someone absolute and perpetual power to dispose of all possessions,

*L82, B4 adds, "then it is a perfect transfer free of all conditions."

†"it [the people] has transferred all its power to him [the emperor]" *Dig.*, I, 4 (*de constitutionibus principum*), 1.

‡L82, C2–4 adds, "Yet for important matters within his jurisdiction, a magistrate's ratification is not made retroactive, as is the prince's, whose power in the commonwealth is supreme."

persons, and the entire state at his pleasure, and then to leave it to anyone he pleases, just as a proprietor can make a pure and simple gift of his goods for no other reason than his generosity. This is a true gift because it carries no further conditions, being complete and accomplished all at once, whereas gifts that carry obligations and conditions are not authentic gifts. And so sovereignty given to a prince subject to
{354} obligations and conditions is properly not sovereignty or absolute power.

This does not apply if the conditions attached at the creation of a prince are of the law of God or nature (*la loy de Dieu ou de nature*),[16] as was done after the death of a Great King of Tartary. The prince and* the people, to whom the right of election belongs, choose any relative of the deceased they please, provided that he is a son or nephew, and after seating him on a golden throne, they† pronounce these words, "We beg you, and also wish and bid you, to reign over us." The king then says, "If that is what you want of me, you must be ready to do as I command, and whom I order killed must be killed forthwith and without delay, and the whole kingdom must be entrusted to me and put into my hands." The people answers, "So be it." Then the king, continuing, says, "The word that I speak shall be my sword," and all the people applaud him. After that he is taken hold of, removed from his throne, and set on the ground seated on a bench, and the princes address him in these words: "Look up [129] and acknowledge God, and then look at this lowly bench on which you sit. If you govern well, you will have your every wish; otherwise you will be put down so low and so completely stripped, that even this bench on which you sit will not be left to you." This said, he is lifted on high, and acclaimed king of the Tartars. This power is absolute and sovereign, for it has no other condition than what is commanded by the law of God and of nature.[17]

We can also see that this formula, or one like it, is sometimes used in kingdoms and principalities that descend by right of succession. But there is none quite like the ceremony in Carinthia. Here, in a meadow near the city of Saint Vitus, one can still see a marble rock
{355} which is mounted by a peasant, to whom this office belongs by right of succession, with a black cow on his right, a skinny mare on his left, and the people all around. The person coming forward to be the duke

* "prince and the" is omitted at L83, A6.

† L83, A8 assigns the speech that follows to "the bishop (*pontifex*)."

walks amidst a great number of lords dressed in red, with ensigns carried in front of him, and everything in good order except for the duke, who is dressed like a poor shepherd and carries a crook. The man standing on the rock calls out in Slavic, "Who is this who walks so proudly?" The people answer that he is their prince. Then the peasant asks, "Is he a [true] judge? Does he seek the welfare of the country? Is he of free status, worthy of honor, respectful of religion?" They answer, "He is, and will be." Then the peasant gives the duke a light blow, and the peasant now becomes exempt from all public burdens, while the duke climbs up on the rock brandishing his sword and, speaking to the people, promises to be just. Still in shepherd's dress he goes to Mass, then assumes a ducal garb and returns to the rock to receive homages and oaths of fealty. But it is true that in olden times the duke of Carinthia was only the Grand Huntsman of the [German] emperor (1331), and after the Empire fell into the hands of the House of Austria, to which the duchy belongs, the title of Huntsman and the ancient form of investiture were abolished and the duchies of Carinthia, Styria, Croatia, as well as the counties of Cilli (*Cilie*) and Tyrol were annexed to the duchy of Austria.[18]

Despite what is written about the kingdom of Aragon, the ancient procedure that they used for the kings of Aragon is no longer followed unless the king assembles the Estates, as I have learned from a Spanish knight.* The procedure used to be that the great magistrate,
56} whom they call **[130]** the justice of Aragon,[19] addressed the king in these words:

> *Nos qui valemos tanto come vos, y podemos mas que vos, vos elegimos Re con estas y estas conditiones entra vos y nos, un que mande mas que vos.* That is, "We who count as much as you, and can do more than you, elect you king on such and such conditions between you and us, that there is one whose command is more powerful than yours."

The person who, on the strength of this, wrote that the king was then elected by the people is mistaken, since nothing of that sort ever happened.[20] For it is quite certain that Sanctius the Great conquered the kingdom by right of the stronger from the Moors who had held it for seven hundred years, and that his posterity, male and female, have held the kingdom ever since by right of succession in the closest

* "unless the king . . . Spanish knight" is omitted at L84, A3.

relative. And Pedro Belluga of Aragon, who has provided a painstaking account of the law of Aragon [in his *Speculum principum*], wrote that the people has no right to elect a king unless there is a failure of the line.

It is also impossible and contradictory that the king of Aragon should have less power than the Estates of Aragon, since the same author, Belluga, says that the Estates cannot assemble unless there is an express command of the king, and that once assembled they cannot leave if it does not please the king to let them go. It is still more ridiculous to believe that such words [in the alleged ceremony] were spoken to a king who had already been crowned, consecrated, and acknowledged as king by right of succession and who, since he was indeed the sovereign, gave the person called the great justice of
{*357*} Aragon his office, and removed him from it as he pleased. In fact the same author [Belluga] writes that Martin Didato was installed and removed from this office by the queen of Aragon in the absence of her husband, Alphonso, king of Aragon and Sicily.

Although by the king's sufferance the justice of Aragon judges suits and controversies between the king and the people – which is something that is also done in England, either by the upper house (*haute chambre*) of Parliament or by the magistrate they call the {chief} justice of England, and by all judges in this kingdom and in every part of it – still the justice of Aragon and all the Estates together remain in complete subjection to the king. As the same doctor says, the king is in no way bound to follow their advice or to grant their requests, which is the rule for all true monarchies, for they have absolute power, as Oldrado said, speaking of the kings of France and Spain.[21]

[131] Yet these doctors do not say what absolute power is. For if we say that to have absolute power is not to be subject to any law at all, no prince of this world will be sovereign, since every earthly prince is subject to the laws of God and of nature and to various human laws that are common to all peoples.[22] On the other hand, it can happen that a subject is dispensed and exempted from all the laws, ordinances, and customs of his commonwealth, and yet is not a prince or sovereign. We have an example of this in Pompey the Great, who was dispensed from the laws for five years by an express ordinance of
{*358*} the Roman people published at the request of the tribune Gabinius. Nor was this dispensing of a subject from obedience to the laws anything strange or new, since the Senate sometimes gave dispensa-

tions without a recommendation by the people up until the adoption of the Cornelian law, which was published at the request of a tribune. It was now decreed that no one could be exempted from the force of the law, or be given dispensation, by the Senate unless there were at least two hundred senators {present}. For although it was [already] forbidden on pain of death by the law of the Twelve Tables to grant any privilege unless in the great assembly of the people {*comitia centuriata*}, this law was ill enforced.* However this may be, a subject who is exempted from the force of the laws always remains in subjection and obedience to those who have the sovereignty. But persons who are sovereign must not be subject in any way to the commands of someone else and must be able to give the law to subjects, and to suppress or repeal disadvantageous laws and replace them with others – which cannot be done by someone who is subject to the laws or to
{59} persons having power of command over him.†

This is why the law says that the prince is not subject to the law; and in fact the very word "law" in Latin implies the command of him who has the sovereignty.[23] And so we see that in all edicts and ordinances the clause is added, "notwithstanding all edicts and ordinances from which we have derogated and do derogate[24] by these presents" along with a derogation of [previous] derogatory clauses (*et à la derogatoire des derogatoires*)."‡ This clause was always added in

*For "But this law was ill enforced" L84, D12 substitutes, "But that law had been amended by the Senate."

†For "However this may be . . . power of command over him" L84, D12–85, B1 substitutes, "Someone who is exempted from a single law, or many laws, or all the laws is still bound by the authority of those who have the rights of sovereignty. This applies even if he is exempted from every law of his country indefinitely, as was Augustus who, even though he was *princeps* of the Roman people – that is, the first person of the commonwealth – pretended to be below the people taken collectively in whom the commonwealth's sovereignty lay. For the most part, accordingly, he brought his legislative proposals to the people since it was the people not Augustus who made law, and when it came to electing magistrates, he shook the hands of citizens by way of recommending his candidates to the people. But someone who holds the rights of sovereignty should not be bound by the command of any other person, a point that was put very pithily by Tiberius when he told the Senate, 'The only reason this can have is that none is given (*Non aliter ratio constat, quam si nulli reddatur*).' He was speaking of the sovereign right of giving law not only to individuals, but to all collectively, and of abrogating laws already made, which cannot be done by someone who is bound by the commands and orders of another."

The quotation of Tiberius is from Tacitus, *Annales*, I, 6. As McRae [91, n.] points out, the source has *uni* rather than *nulli* (which may or may not change the meaning of a cryptic remark).

‡*et à la derogatoire des derogatoires* is omitted at L85, B6. The meaning of the French seems unclear.

ancient laws, whether the law {to be amended} had been published by the same prince or by his predecessor. For it is well known that the laws, ordinances, letters patents, privileges [132], and concessions of princes, have force only during their lifetimes unless they are ratified by the express consent, or at least the sufferance, of a prince who is cognizant of them. This especially applies to privileges. This explains why Bartolus [de Saxoferrato], when he was sent on an embassy to the emperor Charles IV to obtain confirmation of the privileges of Perugia, obtained the confirmation, but with the clause included, "Until such time as they may be revoked by our successors," since he [Charles] could do nothing to prejudice their rights.* This was the reason why Michel de l'Hôpital, the chancellor of France, refused to
{360} seal the confirmation of privileges and exemptions from tailles of Saint-Maure-les-Fossés, even though he had been ordered to do it {by Charles IX}. It was because they conferred a perpetual exemption, which is contrary to the nature of personal privileges and diminishes the power of successor princes. And privileges cannot be given to corporations and guilds except for the lifetime of the prince who grants them, even if the word perpetual is used, which it never is in the democratic and aristocratic states.[25] This is why the emperor Tiberius, Augustus' successor, ordered that privileges granted by deceased emperors should not have any effect if their successors had not confirmed them. For, as Suetonius reports, those who had been given privileges wanted to have their exemptions taken as perpetual unless the grant had been [expressly] limited to a definite period of time. We also see that upon the advent of a new king in this kingdom, all the guilds and communities ask for confirmation of their privileges, powers, and jurisdictions – the Parlements and sovereign courts[26] as well as particular officials.

If the sovereign prince is thus exempt from the laws of his predecessors, much less is he bound by laws and ordinances that he has made himself. For although one can receive law from someone else, it is as impossible by nature to give one's self a law as it is to command
{361} one's self to do something that depends on one's own will. As the law says, *Nulla obligatio consistere potest, quae a voluntate promittentis statum capit*† – which is a rational necessity and clearly demonstrates that a king cannot be subject to the laws. Just as the pope never ties his

*L85, C2 adds, "even if this clause had not been added."

†"No obligation can exist that depends on the will of the person promising."

hands, as the canonists say, so a sovereign prince cannot tie his hands even if he wished to do so. Thus **[133]** at the end of edicts and ordinances we see the words, "for such is our pleasure (*car tel est nostre plaisir*)," which serve to make it understood that the laws of a sovereign prince, even if founded on good and strong reasons, depend solely on his own free will.

But as for divine and natural laws, every prince on earth is subject to them, and it is not in their power to contravene them unless they wish to be guilty of treason against God, and to war against Him beneath whose grandeur all the monarchs of this world should bear the yoke and bow the head in abject fear and reverence. The absolute
62} power of princes and of other sovereign lordships (*seigneuries souverains*), therefore, does not in any way extend to the laws of God and of nature. Indeed he (Innocent IV) who best understood what absolute power is, and made {Christian} kings and emperors bow to him, said that it is nothing but the power of overriding ordinary law. He did not say the laws of God and of nature.

But is the prince not subject to those laws of the land that he has sworn to keep? Here we must distinguish. If the prince swears to himself that he will keep his own law, he is not bound by that law any more than by an oath made to himself. For even subjects are in no way bound by the oath they take in making contracts of a sort that the law permits them to ignore even when the terms are honest and reasonable.[27] And if a sovereign prince promises another prince to keep laws that he or his predecessors have made, he is obligated to keep them if the prince to whom he gave his word has an interest in his so doing – and even if he did not take an oath. But if the prince to whom the promise was made does not have an interest, neither the promise nor the oath can obligate the prince who made the promise.* The same may be said of a promise given to a subject by the prince either when he is sovereign or before he is elected, for in this [latter] respect his status makes no difference, despite what many think.

It is not that the prince is bound by his own or his predecessors'
63} laws, but rather by the just contracts and promises that he has made,

* L86, C2–6 adds, "And although Alessandro Tartagni held in almost all his commentaries and *responsa* that contracts which would otherwise not be binding acquire force solely by virtue of having been sworn to (an opinion that cannot be supported either by probable argument or authority), even he denied that princes were bound by their own decrees and laws even though they had ratified them with an oath."

whether with or without an oath, as is any private individual. And just as a private individual can be relieved of a promise that is unjust or unreasonable, or burdens him too much, or was put upon him to his substantial loss through trickery, fraud, error, force, [134] or reasonable fear, so for the same reasons can a prince, if he is sovereign, be relieved of anything that involves a diminution of his majesty. And so our maxim stands. The prince is not subject to his own laws or to the laws of his predecessors, but only to his just and reasonable contracts in the observation of which his subjects in general or particular subjects have an interest.

Here many commentators mistakenly confuse the prince's laws with his contracts, which they call laws, and mistaken also is he [Pedro Belluga] who takes what are called compacted laws (*loix pactionees*) in the Estates of Aragon to be contracts of the prince. When the king makes an ordinance at the request of the Estates and receives money for it, or a subsidy, they say that the king is bound by it, and as for other laws that he is not bound. Nevertheless they admit that the prince can override it if the reason for the law should cease. This is
{*364*} true enough, and well founded in reason and authority. But there is no need for money and an oath to oblige a sovereign ruler if the subjects to whom he has given his promise have an interest in the law being kept. For the word of the prince should be like an oracle, and his dignity suffers when one has so low an opinion of him that he is not believed unless he swears, or is not [expected to be] faithful to his promises unless one gives him money. Nevertheless the force of the legal maxim still remains. A sovereign prince can override a law that he has promised and sworn to keep if it ceases to be just without the consent of his subjects, although it is true that in this case a general derogation does not suffice unless a special derogation goes along with it.[28] But if there is no just cause to set aside a law that he has promised to maintain, the prince ought not and cannot [justly] contravene it.[29]

On the other hand, he is not bound to the contracts and oaths of his predecessors unless he is their heir.* And this is the ground on which

* To "unless he is their heir," L87, B1–2 adds, "except in so far as he has profited from them," which helps the transition. But even so the transition is misleading. The point of this paragraph is that even where an incumbent is obligated by the promises of a predecessor, he may for good reason alter legislation unilaterally. On obligations stemming from the acts of predecessors, see below, pp. 42–45.

the Estates of Aragon complained to King Alphonso that he had changed and altered the money of Aragon to gain a profit, that this was to the extreme disadvantage of his subjects and foreign mer-
{55} chants, and that it was contrary to a promise made by James I, king of Aragon, in April 1265 and confirmed by King Peter in 1336, who swore to the Estates that he would never alter the money. For this the people, by way of recompense, [135] promised the king one *maravedis* per hearth every seven years to be paid by all those whose worth came to fifteen *maravedis*, [a coin] which is equal to half a *liard*.[30] Now it is clear that the kingdom of Aragon goes by heredity to males and also to females; yet the purpose of the convention between the prince and the people ceasing, as well as of the subsidy for which the kings of Aragon passed the ordinance that I have mentioned, the prince is no longer bound by it, any more than the people are bound to pay the subsidy imposed if the prince does not keep his promise.*

It is essential, therefore, not to confuse a law and a contract. Law depends on him who has the sovereignty and he can obligate all his subjects {by a law} but cannot obligate himself. A contract between a prince and his subjects is mutual; it obligates the two parties reciprocally and one party cannot contravene it to the prejudice of the other and without the other's consent. In this case the prince has no advantage over the subject except that, if the justice of a law that he has sworn to keep ceases, he is no longer bound by his promise, as we
{56} have said, which is a liberty that subjects cannot exercise with respect to each other unless they are relieved [of their obligations] by the prince.

Furthermore, sovereign† princes who are well informed never take an oath to keep the laws of their predecessors, or else they are not sovereign.[31] Someone will object, perhaps, that, before he is consecrated, the emperor, who has precedence over all other Christian kings, swears in the hands of the archbishop of Cologne to keep the laws of the Empire and the Golden Bull; to establish justice; to obey the pope;‡ to maintain the Catholic faith; and to defend widows, orphans, and the poor. That in sum is the oath that Charles V took and which was sent to the pope by Cardinal Cajetan, the papal ambas-

*"any more . . . keep his promise" is omitted at L87, C2.
†"sovereign" is omitted at L87, C10.
‡For "obey the pope" L87, D6 substitutes "courteously respect the sovereignty of the pope."

sador in Germany. But I answer that the emperor is subject to the Estates of the Empire, and does not claim sovereignty over the princes or the Estates, as we will point out in due course.

And if someone says that the kings of the Epirotes in ancient times swore they would reign well and properly according to the laws of the land, and that the subjects also swore, reciprocally, that they would keep and maintain the king according to the ordinances and customs of the country, I say that these oaths notwithstanding, a sovereign prince can modify the laws, and even repeal or annul them, if they cease to be just.* But the oath of our kings, which is **[136]** the most beautiful and most concise that can be devised, includes nothing about keeping the laws and customs of the country or their predecessors. I shall set it down word for word exactly as extracted from an old book in the library of Reims, which begins:

{*367*} *Iuliani ad Erigium Regem, Anno MLVIII, Henrico regnante XXXII. III Calend, Iunii: . . . Ego Philippus Deo propiciante mox futurus Rex Francorum, in die ordinationis meae, promitto coram Deo et sanctis eius, quod unicuique de nobis commissis canonicum privilegium et debitam legem atque iustitiam conservabo, et defensionem, adiuvante Domino, quantum potero exhibebo, sicut Rex in suo regno unicuique Episcopo, et ecclesia sibi commissae per rectum exhibere debet: populo quoque nobis credito, me dispensationem legum in suo iure consistentem, nostra auctoritate concessurum. Qua perlecta posuit eam in manus Archiepiscopi.*†

* "And if someone says . . . cease to be just." L87, D11–L88, A4, in a major shift of interpretation, removes the obvious inconsistency here and compares the Epirote kings to the German Emperors. "Similarly, the kings of the [ancient] Epirotes, upon taking office, used to swear that they would observe the laws of the country, and their subjects also swore that they would carry out the prince's commands according to the laws and customs of their ancestors. For although the title king is august and sacred, many have it in name only and not in fact, as is reported of the kings of Denmark and Bohemia. And we will reach the same conclusion on the kings of the Epirotes."

† [From] Julianus to Master (*Regem*) Erigius in the year 1058, the thirty-second in the reign of Henry I, on the twenty-ninth day of May: . . . I, Philip, God willing, about to become king of the French, do promise before God and His saints on this day of my coronation to secure canonical privilege, due law, and justice to every person entrusted to our charge and, with God's help, I will provide for their defense so far as I am able, as a king in his kingdom rightly ought to do for every bishop and church committed to his care. And to the people entrusted to our care, [I promise] that I will grant by our authority execution of the laws consistent with their right. After this was read he placed it in the hands of the archbishop.

I have also learned that the oath found in the library of Beauvais is very similar and is by the same King Philip I.

But I have seen another version of our oath, in a very old little book in the abbey of St. Allier in Auvergne,* which reads, "I swear in the name of almighty God and I promise to govern well and duly the subjects committed to my care, and with all my strength to give (*faire*) judgment, justice, and mercy." This seems to be taken from Jeremiah [9, (24)] where it is said, "I am the great God eternal who gives (*fay*) judgment, justice, and mercy, and in these things I take special delight." This shows at a glance that the oaths contained in a printed book {recently} published on the coronation ceremony entitled *Sacre du Roy* have been much changed and altered from their ancient form. But one can see in either [of the above] version[s] of the oath that there is no obligation to keep the laws unless right and justice would be affected adversely (*sinon tant que le droit et la justice souffrira*).† Indeed it seems that the ancient kings of the Hebrews did not take any oath at all, not even those who were consecrated by Samuel, Elijah, and others.

But some kings take a more restrictive oath (*serment plus precis*) like the oath of Henry III, king of France and Poland, which runs as follows:

> *Ego Henricus Rex Poloniae, etc. iuro Deo omnipotenti, quod omnia iura, libertates, privilegia publica et privata, iuri communi non con-*
> 8} *traria, ecclesiis, principibus, baronibus, nobilibus, civibus, incolis per meos praedecessores Reges, etc. quoscunque principes dominos regni Poloniae iuste donata, ab ordinibusque tempore interregni statuta, sancta, nobis oblata, observabo,* [137] *etc. iustitiamque omnibus incolis iuxta iura publica admnistrabo. Et si (quo absit) sacramentum meum violavero, nullam nobis incolae regni obedientiam praestare debebunt, etc. sic me Deus adiuvet.*‡

* For "But I have seen . . . Auvergne" L88, B6–9 substitutes, "Both these oaths have a priestly aroma about them. But I have copied, from the very ancient archives of a library in Auvergne, the purest and best form of oath that can be devised and I recommend it for all kings to admire and imitate."

† "unless right and justice would be affected adversely" is omitted at L88, C6.

‡ I, Henry, king of Poland etc., swear by almighty God that I will observe all rights, liberties, and privileges public and private not contrary to common law that have been justly granted to churches, princes, barons, nobles, citizens, and inhabitants by the kings my predecessors or by any princes who were lords of the kingdom of Poland, including those established, confirmed, and presented to us by the Estates during the interregnum;

As for laws which concern the state of the kingdom and its basic form, since these are annexed and united to the crown like the Salic law, the prince cannot detract from them. And should he do so, his successor can nullify anything that has been done in prejudice of the royal laws on which the sovereign majesty is founded and supported.*

One might still object that when Henry V, king of France and England, married Catherine of France, the sister of Charles VII, he swore that he would maintain the Parlement in its liberties and sovereign prerogatives, and that he would administer justice in the kingdom in accordance with its rights and customs. The words here are from the treaty, entered into on 21 May 1420, naming a successor to the crown of France. My answer is that they made him take this oath because he was a stranger coming to a new kingdom, the legitimate successor {Charles VII} having been set aside by a decree of the Parlement of Paris, with Charles absent and in contempt, because of the murder of John of Burgundy, which decree was pronounced at the marble table in the presence of the princes and with the sound of a trumpet.[32]

But as to general and local customs that do not concern the foundations of the kingdom, it is the custom not to change anything in them without having duly assembled the Three Estates of France as a whole, or of each *bailliage* in particular.† But this does not mean that their advice must be taken, or that the king cannot do the opposite of what is asked if natural reason and the justice of what he wants
{369} support him. It is thus that the grandeur and majesty of a truly sovereign prince is manifested – when the Estates of all the people are

and that I will administer justice to all inhabitants in accordance with established public law. And if (may it never come to pass) I should violate my oath, the inhabitants of the kingdom shall not be bound to render me obedience, etc., so help me God. L84, D8–9 adds, "This points not to royal sovereignty but to the status of a [mere] prince (that is, of someone who is [merely] first in the state)." (On the principate, see below, p. 107.)

*L88, D12–L89, A2 introduces a significant elaboration, "And if there is any detraction from these fundamental laws (*leges imperii*), the magistrates normally correct it once the prince is dead. They will not acknowledge any decree of his that goes against the fundamental laws, such as a diminution of the rights of sovereignty or a usurpation of the commonwealth's domain." (Thus an act against fundamental law by a previous king may be disallowed by the magistrates upon his death without an act of repeal by the successor.)

†L89, B2–3 omits mention of the Estates-General and speaks only of the "convocation of the Estates of each community (*cuiusque civitatis ordinibus convocatis*)." This, however, may have been an oversight, since the consultation of the Estates-General as ordinary practice is implied in the paragraphs that follow.

assembled and present requests and supplications to their prince in all humility, without having any power to command or decree, or even a right to deliberate (*ny voix deliberative*), and whatever the king pleases by way of consent or dissent, command or prohibition, is taken for law, for edict, or for ordinance.

Hence those who have written on the duty of magistrates and other such books are mistaken in holding that the Estates of the people are **[138]** greater than the prince.[33] It is an opinion that leads subjects to revolt from the obedience they owe their sovereign prince, and there is neither reason nor any basis whatsoever for it unless the king is a captive or insane. For if a sovereign prince is subject to the Estates, he is neither prince nor sovereign, and the state is neither a kingdom nor a monarchy, but a pure aristocracy[34] of many lords with equal power, where the greater part commands the smaller part collectively, and each individual particularly. Edicts and ordinances would then have to be issued in the name of the Estates, and be commanded by them as in an aristocracy where the person who presides has no power and has to obey the orders of the governing body – all of which is absurd and inconsistent [in a monarchy].*

Thus at the assembly of the Estates of this kingdom held at Tours [1484], at a time when King Charles VIII was under age and the Estates had more authority than ever, we see Relli, the orator who spoke for all of the Estates, begin his speech as follows:

> Most high, most powerful, and most Christian king, our sovereign and natural lord. Your humble and most obedient sub-

*The French edition of 1579, octavo, Jacques du Puy, p. 137 (and this edition only, according to McRae, p. 95, note E6) adds: "and also pernicious. And on this pretext [of the people's superiority] there are some who have sought to make the kingdom elective, with power in the Estates to take sceptres and crowns away from the true successors in order to give them to the most factious and ambitious. This inevitably brings with it the ruin of kingdoms that were founded on a rule of succession as their solid foundation, as I pointed out at the Estates of France held at Blois in 1576 which I attended as a deputy sent by the Estates of Vermandois. For it is quite certain that the people as a whole can only petition, that the privy council can only deliberate, and that those who attend the privy council without having a seat in it can only give advice, while the king alone decides. For if it were otherwise, and the decision were in the hands of many, the marks of sovereignty would disappear, and the monarchy would be no more than an aristocracy or a democracy exposed to the dangerous scheming of the most mischievous and factious." (Bodin does not reject election as inherently incompatible with the principle of monarchy, but only the idea that the power to elect entails a power to depose. His target here could well be François Hotman's *Francogallia* [1st ed., 1573], which asserted that connection.)

> jects, convened here by your command, appear before you and present themselves to you in all humility, reverence, and subjection, etc. And I have been charged by everyone in this noble assembly to express to you their good wishes, cordial affection, and firm determination to serve and obey you, and to give you support in all of your affairs, commands, and wishes.

In brief, in all of the speeches and discussions of the Estates there is nothing but subjection, service, and obedience. And the same applies to the Estates of Orléans [1560].

Nor can one say that they do differently in Spain. For the same expressions of submission and subjection, service and obedience, on the art of the entire people to the king of Spain as to their sovereign lord, may be found in the speeches of the Estates held at Toledo in 1552. Here too we find replies of the sovereign prince to the humble requests and petitions of the people with the words "We will" or "We have ordered," along with other responses of this sort bearing the prince's refusal or agreement. Indeed, the very tax that the people pay to the king of Spain is called "the service." Hence **[139]** Pedro Belluga was mistaken when he said that the kings of Aragon cannot detract from the privileges of the Estates, in view of the privilege granted to them by King James in 1260 and confirmed in 1320. For just as the privilege ceased to be valid on the death of James I without confirmation by his successor, so the same confirmation by the other [and still later] kings is necessary in accordance with the legal maxim that one equal cannot command another (*qui ne souffre pas qu'on puisse commander à son pareil*).

{*371*} Although in the Parliaments of the kingdom of England, which they hold every three years, the Estates assume a greater liberty, as is the wont with peoples of the north, yet in fact they too proceed only by supplication and request. In the English Parliament held in October 1560, all the Estates by common agreement had resolved, and gave the queen to understand, that they would not take up any business until she named a successor to the crown. She replied that they were looking to dig her grave before she died, but that all their resolutions would be of no effect without her will; and she did not do anything they asked, as I have learned from the letters of the English ambassador. Moreover, the Estates of England are never assembled, any more than are those of this kingdom or of Spain, but by letters patent and express commands emanating from the king, which clearly shows that the Estates have no power of deciding, commanding, or determining anything, seeing that they cannot meet or dissolve without an express command.

One might still say that ordinances made by the king of England at the request of the Estates cannot be repealed without calling the Estates. That is the common practice, and it is what is ordinarily done, as I have learned from Mr. Dale, the English ambassador, an honorable and learned man. But he has assured me that the king accepts or rejects laws as he sees fit, and does not hesitate to ordain law at his pleasure and against the will of the Estates, as did Henry VIII, who always invoked his sovereign power. For although the kings of England are not consecrated unless they swear to keep the ordinances and customs of the country, that oath must be related to what we have said above.[35]

[140] But someone may object that the Estates* do not tolerate the imposition of extraordinary levies or subsidies unless they are granted and consented to in Parliament, in accordance with a decree of Henry I in the great charter,† a document in virtue of which the
2} people have always prevailed against their kings. My answer is that other kings have no more power than the king of England. For there is no prince in all the world who has the power to levy taxes on the people at his pleasure any more than he has the power to take another's goods,[36] as Philippe de Commines wisely remonstrated at the Estates of Tours [1484] in a speech reported in his memoirs. If the need is urgent, the prince ought not to wait for the Estates to meet[37] or for the consent of the people, since its welfare depends on the foresight and diligence of a wise prince. And we will speak of this in due course.[38] But it is true that the kings of England, beginning with Henry I as we read in Polydore [Virgil],[39] have customarily asked for an extraordinary subsidy[40] every three years and have almost always received it. Thus at the Parliament that met in April 1570, the queen of England obtained the equivalent of 500,000 gold crowns (*escus*) by consent of the Estates. And they‡ do the same in the Spanish Estates.

*L90, D8 mentions the Spanish Estates along with the English.
†For "a decree of Henry I in the great charter" L90, D8 substitutes, "an ancient law of Henry I." (This charter of the early twelfth century was taken as a precedent by the authors of *Magna Charta*, and Bodin seems to have run the two together in the French.)
‡L91, A8 adds "sometimes."

Here someone may object that the Estates of England have the power to punish. Thus Thomas and Henry Howard were condemned by the Estates at the indictment (*poursuite*) of King Henry VIII of England, and, even more remarkable, King Henry VI was also sentenced by the Estates to be imprisoned in the Tower of London.[41] But I answer that this was done by the ordinary judges of England [seated] in the upper house of Parliament at the request of the lower house, which also presented a request to the upper house in 1571 for a determination that the Counts of Northumberland, Westmorland, and other conspirators had incurred the penalties established by the law of the land for the crime of treason. This clearly shows that the
{*373*} Estates as a body have neither power nor jurisdiction, but that the power lies in the judges of the upper house.* It would be as if the Parlement of Paris, assisted by the princes and the peers, were present as a separate body in the Estates to judge great cases.

One difficulty concerning the Estates of England still remains to be resolved **[141]**, in that they seem to be empowered to command, resolve, and decide in great affairs of state. For when Queen Mary had them assembled to verify (*faire passer*) the articles dealing with her marriage to King Philip [of Spain], many disputes and difficulties were raised before the treaty was finally verified on 2 April 1554. The verification was in the form of a decree issued in the name of the Estates and in these words:

> The above articles and that which depends on them having been examined by the Estates assembled in the Parliament met at Westminster Palace, it is declared: As for the disposition and conferment of all benefices and offices, they are reserved to the queen, as also all the fruits, profits, rents, and revenues of her countries, lands, and lordships (*seigneuries*); and the queen alone and of herself shall enjoy the royalty and sovereignty of the said kingdoms, countries, lands, and subjects, absolutely after the consummation of the marriage: without the said prince being able to pretend, by the form of the courtesy of England,† to the crown and sovereignty of the kingdom, or to any other right, preeminence, or authority. [It is also declared] that all mandates and letters patent shall pass under the name of the said prince and the queen conjointly; which letters signed by the hand of the

*L91, B9 calls these "extraordinary judges appointed by the king."

†Bodin note to p. 141, "by which the husband is usufructuary of his wife's goods if he survives her."

queen alone and sealed with the great seals of the chancellory, shall be valid: but if they are not signed by the said queen they shall be void.

I have chosen to quote this verification at length to show that the entire sovereignty belongs undivided to the kings of England and that the Estates are only witnesses. For verification by the Estates, no more than verification by a court, a Parlement, a corporation, or a
4} guild, does not suffice to show power to command. It is rather consent to the validity of acts, on which some doubt might otherwise be cast after the queen was dead, or even while she lived, by opposition from the magistrates and officers of the kingdom.[42]

We shall conclude, then, that the sovereignty of the monarch is in no way altered by the presence of the Estates. On the contrary, his majesty is all the greater and more illustrious when all his people publicly acknowledge him as sovereign, even though, in an assembly like this, princes, not wishing to rebuff their subjects, grant and pass many things that they would not consent to [142] had they not been overcome by the requests, petitions, and just complaints of a harassed and afflicted people which has most often been wronged without the knowledge of the prince, who sees and hears only through the eyes, ears, and reports of others.

We thus see that the main point of sovereign majesty and absolute power consists of giving the law to subjects in general without their consent. Not to go to other countries, we in this kingdom have often seen certain general customs repealed by edicts of our kings without hearing from the Estates when the injustice of the rules was obvious (*oculaire*).* Thus the custom concerning the inheritance by mothers of their children's goods, which was observed in this kingdom throughout the entire region governed by customary law,[43] was changed without assembling either the general or local estates.† Nor is this something new. In the time of King Philip the Fair, the general custom of the entire kingdom, by which the losing party in a [civil] case could not be required to pay [court] expenses, was suppressed by an edict without assembling the Estates. And the general custom that
5} prohibited the taking of testimony from women in civil cases was repealed by an edict of Charles VI [in 1394] without calling the

* "when . . . obvious" is omitted at L92, A9, perhaps because it seemed to Bodin, on second thoughts, to suggest conditions on the power to repeal.

† "Thus the custom . . . local Estates" is omitted at L92, A9.

Estates. For a sovereign prince has to have the laws in his power in order to change and correct them according to the circumstances; just as the master pilot, said the jurist Sextus Caecilius, ought to have the rudder in his hand to move at his discretion if the ship is not to go down while waiting on the opinion of its passengers.

This is necessary not only for the sovereign prince, but sometimes also for the magistrate, as we have said of Pompey and the Decemvirs. That is why Augustus, after the battle of Actium, was exempted from the laws by the Senate, even though he was only the chief person of the state rather than a sovereign prince, as we shall explain in due course. After Vespasian, furthermore, the emperor was also exempted from the laws by what many think was an express law of the people that is still to be found at Rome engraved in stone and is called the royal law {*lex regia*}[44] by the jurists. But it is not very likely that the people, who had lost all their power long before, now gave it to the stronger party.*

{*376*} But if it is useful for a **[143]** sovereign prince to have power over the laws in order to govern well, it is even more expedient for the governing body in an aristocracy; while for the people in a democracy, it is a logical necessity (*necessaire*). For the monarch is separate from the people, and in an aristocracy the nobles are separate from the commoners. Hence in the one as in the other there are two parties – the person or persons that have the sovereignty on the one side, and the people on the other – which causes the difficulties that arise between them on the rights of sovereignty. But these disappear in a democracy. For if the prince or the nobles (*seigneurs*) who are in possession of the state are obligated to keep the laws, as many think, and cannot make law without the permission of the people or the Senate, then a law can also not be changed, legally speaking, without the consent of both parties – which cannot happen in a democracy since the people is but one body and cannot obligate itself.

Why then, it will be asked, did the Roman people swear to keep the

*"After Vespasian . . . stronger party." L92, C3–9 is more precise and coherent. "Later on, Vespasian is said to have been exempted from the laws not only by the Senate, but also by the people, and sovereign power to have been transferred to him in its entirety by the royal law (*lege regia*) which is mentioned [in the *Digest*] as having been passed concerning his authority (*imperio*) and which, inscribed in marble, is still extant at Rome. Yet it seems ridiculous to speak of the people passing a royal law since Tiberius had completely removed the rights of assembly and of voting that had been left to the commoners (*plebi*) by Augustus."

laws? Dio [Cassius] writes that this was a new custom introduced at the request of a tribune {Saturninus}, and then continued for all laws even when they were unjust and absurd. But this does not resolve the difficulty. I would say that each person took the oath as an individual,
77} something which all collectively could not have done since an oath, properly speaking, is rendered only by a lesser to a greater. In a monarchy, on the contrary, each individual and the entire people as a body must swear to keep the laws and take an oath of loyalty to the sovereign monarch, who does not himself owe any oath except to God alone, of whom he holds his scepter and his power. For an oath always implies reverence towards the person to whom it is given or in whose name it is taken, which is the only reason why a lord does not take an oath to his vassal even though the obligation between them is mutual.

But if it is true that a sovereign prince owes no oath except to God, why did Trajan take an oath to keep the laws before a consul who remained seated while he stood? The answer is twofold. In the first place, he swore an oath only when he took the consulship and, like every magistrate newly entering an office, swore it on the first day of the new year, after making a sacrifice in the Campidoglio, before the highest magistrate to be found **[144]** in the city. And Trajan sometimes took the consulship in addition to his imperial title, as the other emperors also did. In the second place, the early Roman emperors were not sovereign, but only chiefs and first citizens, who were called *principes*. This form of state, in appearance aristocratic but monarchical in practice, was called a *principatus*.* The emperor's [only] prerogative was to be the first in dignity, honor, and precedence, although in fact the majority of emperors were tyrants. Indeed, one day, when some foreign kings were arguing about their nobility and grandeur at his table, Caligula quoted the verse from Homer, *Ouk agathon hē polukoiraniē eis koiranos estō basileus* – that is to
8} say, "It is not expedient to have many rulers, and there is need for but one king," and he was not very far, says Suetonius, from taking the diadem and changing the form of state, which was a principate, into a kingdom. Now it is clear that in a principate, the captain or prince is

*The definition of a principate is run together in this sentence with a critique of its practice as a sham. The confusion is removed at L93, B2–3 which substitutes, "A principate is understood to be a form of aristocracy in which one person has precedence over all the rest in dignity, as at Venice." The Latin fails, however, to include the possibility that, technically at least, a principate, as Bodin defines it, could also be a form of democracy.

not sovereign, any more than is the duke at Venice, as we shall explain in due course.

But even when one acknowledges that the emperors had effectively usurped sovereignty, as they surely had, it is no surprise that Trajan, who was one of the best princes that ever existed in this world, swore to keep the laws, even though he was exempt in his capacity as prince. It was to provide his subjects with an example of scrupulous observance. And previous to him no emperor had ever done this. This is why Pliny the Younger, speaking of Trajan's oath, exclaimed, "Behold something strange and never seen before: the emperor swearing to keep the laws . . . !" – which shows that it was very new. Theodoric, later, wishing to gain the favor of the Senate and the Roman people, followed Trajan's example, as we read in Cassiodorus. *Ecce*, says Theodoric, *Traiani nostri clarum seculis reparamus exemplum: iurat vobis, per quem iuratis.** And it is likely that other princes have turned this into a custom, and take an oath at their coronation, even when they have the sovereignty by right of succession.[45]

It is true **[145]** no doubt that the kings of northern peoples[46] take oaths that detract from their sovereignty. In fact, the nobility of
{*379*} Denmark held up the coronation of King Frederick [II] in August 1559 until he had solemnly sworn that he would not execute a nobleman or confiscate his property unless the accused had been tried by the Senate; that all gentlemen would have jurisdiction and the power of capital punishment over their subjects without appeal and without the king having any share of fines and confiscations; and that the king would have no power to bestow any office without the consent of the Senate.† All of these are arguments showing that the [present] king of Denmark is not a sovereign. But this is an oath that was initially forced from the lips of Frederick, grandfather of the present Frederick, during his war against King Christian of Denmark, who died in prison at the age of twenty-five; and it was confirmed by Christian, Frederick's father, who took the same oath. And so that he

* "Let it be seen," says Theodoric, "that we are renewing the example of Trajan, which has been famous through the ages. He swears unto you by whom you swear." (The emperor in question is not Theodoric but his successor, Athalaric.)

† For "and that the king . . . consent of the Senate" L93, D13–L94, A1 substitutes, "and that he would not give any honors or offices to private persons but leave it to the determination of the Senate" (which indicates an even more stringent limitation of royal power).

would not be able to break his oath, the nobility concluded an alliance with the city of Lubeck, and also with King Sigismund Augustus of Poland, who had hardly anything more in the way of sovereignty than the king of Denmark.

But it has to be one way or the other. The prince who swears to keep the civil laws either is not sovereign or else becomes a perjurer if he violates his oath, which a sovereign prince will have to do in order to annul, change, or correct the laws according to the exigencies of situations, times, and persons.[47] Or else, if we say that the prince, without ceasing to be sovereign, is still bound to take the advice of the Senate or the people, he will also have to be dispensed by his subjects from the oath he took to keep the laws inviolate; and the subjects who are bound and obligated to the laws, both individually and collectively, will also need a dispensation from the prince on pain of being perjured. Sovereignty will thus be tossed up and back between two parties, and sometimes the people, sometimes the prince will be the master – which are egregious absurdities and utterly incompatible
{30} with absolute sovereignty, as well as contrary to the laws and to natural reason.

Nevertheless, we see highly knowledgeable commentators maintaining that princes should be required to take an oath to keep the laws and customs of the land. [146] By doing this they weaken and degrade sovereign majesty, which should be sacred, and produce an aristocracy, or even a democracy.[48] It also happens that the sovereign prince, seeing that they would steal what is his and subject him to his own laws, exempts himself at last not only from the civil laws, but also from the laws of God and of nature, treating them as all the same.

It is especially important, therefore, to clarify this point. For someone could still object that by the law of the Medes and the Persians, edicts of the king were irrevocable. Even though the king of the Medes wished to exempt Daniel from the capital punishment mandated by the edict he had violated, the princes remonstrated that an edict could not be revoked since that was not permitted by the law of the land. And Daniel was in fact thrown to the lions. If, then, the greatest monarch on earth could not abrogate the edicts he had made, our positions on sovereign power are ill founded. Furthermore, the limitation in question can occur not only in monarchies, but also in a democracy like Athens. Thucydides shows that the Peloponnesian War began because of an edict made by the Athenian people which

removed the right of landing at the port of Athens from the Megarians. After they [the Megarians] lodged a complaint with the allies over this outrage to the law of nations, the Spartans dispatched an embassy to the Athenians to ask them to revoke the edict. Pericles, who was then all-powerful in Athens, replied to the ambassadors that the laws of the Athenians expressly provided that edicts published and hung up on the pillars[49] could never be repealed. If that is true, the
{381} people was bound not only by its own laws, but also by the laws of its predecessors.

Furthermore, the emperor Theodosius decided that edicts should be made with the consent of all the Senators. And in the ordinance of King Louis XI of France concerning the creation of an order of knights, Article 8 expressly states that the king will not undertake wars or any other momentous and dangerous enterprises without informing the knights of the order so that he might hear and make use of their counsel and advice. This also is why the edicts of our kings [147] have no effect unless they are published, verified, and registered in the Parlement* with the consent of the procuror general and the approval of the [high] court. It is also a maxim of English law, invariably observed, that all ordinances affecting the foundations of the state (*portans coup à l'estat*) will be questioned, unless they are authorized by the Parliament of England.

I answer that these objections do not invalidate the rule of public law that we have postulated. As to the [supposed] law of the Medes, it was purely a malicious falsehood (*pure calomnie*) raised against Daniel by courtiers who were offended by the sight of a foreign prince raised up so high in their land and to a rank not far from the king's own majesty. The king went along with it only to see whether the God of Daniel would protect him from the sentence, which He did; whereupon the king had Daniel's enemies thrown into the den of hungry lions, which shows that he was not subject to the civil laws of his country. We can also see this in the fact that Darius Mnemon,[50] acting at the request of a young Jewish lady {Esther}, repealed an edict in which he had ordered the extermination of the Jewish people.
{382} As for Pericles, he was seeking to start a war so that he could escape indictment by his enemies, for so Theopompus and Timaeus attested, and Plutarch did not deny it. That is why he told the Spartan ambas-

* For "the Parlement," L95, B1–2 specifying, or perhaps amending, substitutes "the high court [Parlement] of each province."

sadors that edicts once hung on the pillars could not be removed. But they paid him back in true Laconic fashion, saying that they did not want the edict to be taken down but only to have the tablet turned around.

If the edicts of the Athenians were irrevocable, why do we see an endless train of laws which they made in and out of season to bring in innovations? To prove that Pericles was imposing on the ambassadors, we need only look at the speech delivered by Demosthenes against Leptines, who had laid a proposal before the people asking for a perpetual and irrevocable edict thenceforth forbidding, on pain of death, the presentation of a request to the people for any privilege or exemption, with the same punishment for anyone who should speak in favor of repealing the edict. Demosthenes blocked his proposal on the spot by showing that the people, in granting this edict, would obviously strip itself not only of its prerogative of conferring [148] exemptions and privileges, but also of its power to make and repeal laws as the need arose. In Athens there was also a people's action against infringement of the laws that could be brought against anyone who tried to get the people to pass an edict contrary to the laws already received, as we know from Demosthenes' speeches. But that never prevented good and advantageous new laws from being pre-
83} ferred over old, unjust ones. Similarly, the general edict providing that a fine once adjudged by the people should never be reduced was revoked many times – once, notably, in favor of Pericles, and again in favor of Cleomedon and Demosthenes, each of whom had been condemned by different judgments of the people to a fine of thirty thousand crowns (*escus*). It is also said that in this kingdom a fine once paid, whether justified or not, is never remitted, and yet one often sees the contrary.

It is a mere manner of proceeding, always found in every state, that those who make the laws add such words as "by perpetual and irrevocable edict," in order to give them greater weight and authority. In this kingdom the phrase "to all persons present and future" is put at the beginning of important edicts to indicate their continuing character to posterity. To make the difference even clearer between these edicts and others that are meant to be temporary, they seal the former in green wax with green and red silk ties, the latter [only] in yellow wax.

Nevertheless, none of these edicts are perpetual, any more than they were at Rome, where whoever published a law added at the end that it could not be altered either by the Senate or the people. If that was really effective, why did the people repeal laws from one day to the next? Cicero says:

> You know that the tribune Clodius, in the law that he has published, had it state at the end that neither the Senate nor the people could detract from it in any way. But it is well known that no one has ever paid attention to the clause, *ut nec per Senatum, nec per populum lex infirmari possit.** Were it otherwise, no law would ever be repealed, since there is none that does not bear that clause, which, however, is regularly set aside.†

{*384*} This is even better stated in the speech of Fabius Ambustus against
[149] a veto by the tribunes, who maintained that the people could not choose two nobles as consuls in defiance of the law that required one of them to be a commoner. Fabius said that by the law of the Twelve Tables,[51] the last decree of the people was the strongest.‡

It is thus evident that the Persians, Medes, Greeks, and Latins use the same formula to validate their edicts and ordinances as do our kings, who sometimes affix the clause, "without it being possible hereafter for us or our successors to detract from it," or "without regard to any [future] abrogation which from this time forth we have declared void." Nevertheless, there is simply no way, as we have said, to give one's self a law that one cannot get out of. For the edict made later always bears an express abrogation of the [clause forbidding] abrogations. Solon, not wanting to make the Athenians keep his laws forever, was content to order them to be kept for a hundred years. Yet soon afterwards, while he was still alive and present, he was to see most of them altered.

As for the verification of edicts on the part of the Estates or the Parlement, it is of great importance for making sure that they are kept.

* "that this law cannot be annulled either by the Senate or by the people."

† "Were it otherwise . . . set aside." L96, C8–10, which gives Cicero's language exactly, is more pointed: "*nam si id esse, nulla fere abrogari posset, neque enim ulla est, quae non ipsa se saepiat difficultate abrogationis. Sed cum lex abrogatur, illud ipsum abrogaretur* (For if this were so, almost no law could be repealed since there is none that does not fortify itself by putting up some obstacle to repeal. But when the law is repealed that clause is repealed as well)."

‡ ". . . the last decree of the people was the strongest." L96, D3–4 directly quotes the law as it is given in *Dig.*, I, 3 (*de legibus*), 28; "*Quod postremum iussit populus id ratum esto* (What the people has decreed last, let it be valid)."

But this is not to say that a sovereign prince cannot make law without it. And so Theodosius [II] says *humanum esse* (it is the civilized thing)* to indicate that the consent of the Senate *non tam necessitatis est,*
385} *quam humanitatis.*† And the same applies to the saying that it is seemly for a sovereign prince to keep his own law,‡ for there is nothing that makes him more feared and revered by his subjects, whereas, on the contrary, there is nothing that more abases the authority of his law than his own contempt for it. As an ancient Roman senator said, *Levius est, et vanius sua decreta tollere quam aliorum.*§

But if the prince forbids killing on penalty of death, is he not then bound by his own law? I say that this law is not his law but the law of God and of nature, to which he is more strictly bound than any of his subjects, from which he cannot be dispensed either by the Senate or the people, and for which he is always answerable to the judgment of God, whose inquiry, said Solomon, is very rigorous; and this is why Marcus Aurelius said that magistrates judge private persons; princes, magistrates; and God, princes. Such is the opinion of two princes who have **[150]** always been estimated as among the wisest ever, and I shall add this remark of Antigonus, king of Asia, who hearing a sycophant say that everything is justified for kings, said "Yes! For kings who are barbarians and tyrants." The first to practice this kind of flattery was Anaxarchus towards Alexander the Great, whom he led to believe that the goddess Justice sat on the right hand of Jupiter in order to show
386} that everything princes do is just. But soon afterwards he had occasion to experience that justice, having fallen into the hands of his enemy, the king of Cyprus, who had him broken on an anvil. Seneca said just the opposite: *Caesari cum omnia licent, propter hoc minus licet.*¶

Hence those who state it as a general rule that princes are not subject to their laws, or even to their contracts, give offense to God

*Refers to the opening words of *Cod.* I, 14, 8, which Bodin cites.

†"is not so much of necessity as civility." L97, A7 notes that this remark is an interpretation by Baldus in his commentary, *In omnes Codicis libros, in l. humanum, de legibus* (*Cod.*, I, 14, 8).

‡"it is seemly for a sovereign prince to keep his own law" paraphrases a celebrated line in *Cod.*, I, 14 (*de legib. et const. princ.*), 4, called *l. digna vox*, which Bodin cites in the French and quotes verbatim at L97, A8–9: "*Digna vox maiestate, regnantis legibus alligatum principem se profiteri* (It is an expression worthy of a ruler's majesty for the prince to profess that he is bound by the laws)."

§"It is more capricious and foolish to repeal your own decrees than those of others." L97, B5–6 adds, "Yet it is one thing to do something of one's own accord, quite another to be bound to do it out of obligation."

¶"Caesar, permitted all, is on that account permitted less."

unless they make an exception for the laws of God and of nature and the just contracts and treaties that princes have entered into, or else can point to some special exemption as one does in grants of privilege.* Even Dionysius, the tyrant of Sicily, told his mother that he could readily exempt her from the laws and customs of Syracuse, but not from the laws of nature. And just as the contracts and testaments of private persons cannot detract from the ordinances of magistrates, nor the edicts of magistrates from custom, nor customs from the general laws of a sovereign prince, so the laws of sovereign princes cannot alter or change the laws of God and of nature. This is the reason why Roman magistrates, when they brought requests and laws to the people to be ratified, customarily added this clause at the end: *Si quid ius non esset e.e.l.n.r.* (*eius ea lege nihil rogaretur*), that is to say, if there were anything in it that was not just and reasonable they did not mean to ask it.† There are also many who mistakenly say that a
{*387*} sovereign prince cannot ordain anything against the law of God unless it seems well founded upon reason. But what reason can there be to contravene the law of God {and of nature}? It is even said that someone whom the pope has exempted from divine law is justified before God, against which my appeal is to the truth.

But this objection still remains: if the prince is bound to the laws of nature, and if the civil laws are equitable and reasonable, it follows that princes are also bound to civil law. And this **[151]** relates to what Pacatus said to the emperor Theodosius: *Tantum tibi licet quantum per leges licebit*.‡ I answer that the law of a sovereign prince deals either with a public or a private matter, or with both of these together, and that in any case it looks either to advantage (*proffit*) at the price of honesty (*honneur*),§ or to advantage not involving honesty, or to honesty without advantage, or to advantage joined with honesty, or
{*388*} even to something involving neither advantage nor honesty. When I say honesty (*honneur*), I mean that which is honest according to the laws of nature. It is well settled that to these the prince is obligated, given that such laws are natural even if the prince has had them published; the obligation is even stronger when the law is advantageous as well as just. If a law involves neither advantage nor honesty,

* "... or else ... privilege." This obscure clause is omitted at L97, D9.

† More literally, "If there is anything unjust in it, it is not requested by this law."

‡ "You may do only what the laws allow."

§ The terms in the Latin (98, B4ff.) are *utile* and *honestum*.

it should not be entertained.* If advantage is at odds with honesty, it is only reasonable that honor should prevail. Thus Aristides the Just once said that Themistocles' counsel was highly advantageous to the public and yet was dishonest and indecent.† But even if a law is advantageous and does not breach the rules of natural justice, the prince is not bound to it, but can change or repeal it as seems good to him, provided that his alteration of the law, in giving advantage to some, does not do damage to others without just cause. For the prince can repeal and annul a good ordinance to make way for one not as good or better, since advantage, honesty, and justice admit degrees of more and less. If, then, among advantageous laws, it is permissible for the prince to choose the most advantageous, he may also choose the most equitable and honest laws among those that are just and honest, even if some persons profit and others lose thereby (so long as the gain is to the public and the loss private).‡

But it is not licit for a subject to contravene his prince's laws on the pretext of honesty or justice. Thus, if a prince, in a time of famine, forbids trade in foodstuffs, a prohibition which is not only advantageous to the public but often just and reasonable, he ought not to allow a few individuals to make a good thing of it to the prejudice of the public generally, and of merchants in particular. For under the pretext of [public] gain, which is reaped by flatterers and courtiers, many good merchants suffer loss and the generality of subjects go hungry. Nevertheless, the famine [152] and the scarcity ending, it is still not licit for a subject to contravene his prince's edict if the

* "If a law ... should not be entertained." L98, B10–C2 substitutes and qualifies this: "But if the thing commanded is neither honest nor advantageous, it ought not to be a law; and yet the prince can bind his subjects to laws that he is not obliged to keep, if they do not contain anything improper (*si nihil habeant cum turpitudine coniunctum*)."

† L98, C8–D2 adds, "Here we must make use of ordinary language because we are engaged in a discussion of the commonwealth, which does not lend itself to the subtleties of philosophers. They hold that nothing is advantageous unless it is honest, or honest unless it is also just. But since that way of looking at it has long been obsolete, we have to distinguish between the honest and the advantageous."

‡ "If, then ... the loss private)." L98, D8–13 amends and corrects this: "But if it is licit for the prince to enact the less advantageous of two advantageous proposals, it is also licit for him to adopt the less honest and less just of two honest proposals, and to order the former while forbidding the latter. For even if a law causes loss to some citizens and brings advantage to others, public well-being takes precedence over private in so far as that can be arranged." The Latin thus seems clearer and more consistent than the French in supporting the main theme of the paragraph – that is, that the prince has considerable discretion within the limits of natural law.

{389} prohibition has not been lifted, nor is it for him to base that contravention on [the rule of] natural equity, which enjoins us to help the foreigner by giving him a share of the goods that God has caused to grow more in one country than in another. For the law that forbids it is stronger than the apparent equity, unless the prohibition was directly contrary to the law of God and of nature.*

Sometimes the civil law will be good, just, and reasonable, and the prince will not be subject to it in any way whatever. When, for example, he forbids the bearing of arms on pain of death in order to put an end to murders and seditions, he ought not to be subject to his law but, on the contrary, should be well armed to protect the good and punish the wicked. We will come to the same judgment [that is, that the prince is not bound] with respect to edicts and ordinances that affect only a part of the community. The justice of these holds only for some persons, or for a certain time, or in a certain place. The same applies to the variety of punishments, which always depends on civil law, even if the prohibition of crimes is of divine and natural law.† To such edicts and ordinances princes are in no way bound unless natural justice is involved. But that ceasing, the prince is not obligated by them, although his subjects continue to be bound until such time as the prince has altered them. For it is the law of God and of nature that we must obey the edicts and ordinances of him to whom God has given power over us, unless his edicts are directly contrary to the law of God, who is above all princes. Just as the sub-vassal owes an oath of fealty to his lord against all others, excepting his sovereign prince,

* "Thus, if a prince . . . to the law of God and of nature." The apparent obscurity of this passage is removed by L99, A1–B2: "Thus if the prince, moved by a famine, prohibits the exportation of necessities – which is not only just but often very necessary – and then accepts money to permit certain private persons to engage in export, even though that does harm to merchants holding a supply of grain and to the commonwealth, it is still illicit for these merchants to export grain until the law is repealed by the prince. And this applies even if the occasion for breaking the law should be extremely great, as, for example, if the commonwealth has all the staples and comforts it needs in abundance, and natural reason moves us to provide for foreigners who are suffering from want and hunger. Unless the prince's interdict plainly violates the laws of God and nature, the strength of the law that forbids is greater than the claim of equity, the appearance of which may be stretched by anyone to satisfy his greed."

† "The same applies . . . natural law." L99, B10–C2 is clearer: "or which deal with punishments, of which we have an endless variety. For although the punishment of crime comes from nature, the stringency or lightness of the penalties depend on human laws and arrangements, by which the prince ought not to be obligated except in so far as they coincide with natural equity."

so the subject owes obedience to his sovereign prince against all others, reserving the majesty of God, who is the absolute lord of all earthly princes.

From this conclusion we can derive another rule of state – namely, that a sovereign prince is bound by the contracts he has made, whether with his subject or with a foreigner. For since he is the guarantor to his subjects of the agreements and mutual obligations
90} that they have entered with one another, there is all the more reason why he must render justice for his own act (*est il debteur de iustice en son faict*). Thus the Parlement of Paris wrote to King Charles IX [153] in March 1563 that his majesty could not unilaterally break the contract between himself and the clergy without the clergy's consent, inasmuch as he had a duty to give justice. And I am reminded of a legal decision affecting princes that ought to be engraved in letters of gold in their caves and palaces (*grottes et Palais*) – namely, that if a prince violates his promise, it should be considered an accident and should not be presumed deliberate. For the obligation of the prince is twofold. It arises on the one hand, from natural equity which requires that agreements and promises be kept and, on the other, from the prince's good faith, which he ought to honor even if he suffers loss because he is the formal guarantor to all his subjects of good faith among themselves, and because there is no crime more detestable in a prince than perjury. That is why less freedom is given to a prince by the law than to his subjects when it is a question of his promise. He cannot take away an office given to his subject without just cause, which a private lord can do, as the courts have ordinarily adjudged. And he cannot take away the fief of his vassal without cause, which other lords can do, according to the principles of feudal law.

91} This will serve to answer the doctors of canon law who have written that a prince can be obliged only in so far as the law of nature requires because, they say, [strict contractual] obligation belongs to civil law.* But this is a mistake because it is a clear and definite principle of jurisprudence that, if contracts belong to natural law or to the common law of peoples, then the obligation and the legal remedy are of the same order. But we would go even further. Even if contracts derive only from civil law, the prince is so strictly obligated by agreements that he makes with his subjects that he cannot impair them

*The canonists cited in the margins are Nicholaus de Tedeschis (Panormitanus), Antonius de Butrio, Ioannes de Imola, Felino Sandeo, and Francesco Zabarella.

even by [invoking] his absolute power, as almost all the doctors of jurisprudence* have agreed.† Indeed, as the master of the Sentences[52] says, God Himself is bound by his promise. "Gather together, He said, all the peoples of the earth that they may judge between my people and Me whether there is anything that I was bound to do and have not done."

{392} That a prince who has contracted with his subjects is bound by his promise should thus be beyond all doubt. But we should not be astonished that some doctors have questioned this, since the jurists have often maintained that a prince is allowed to enrich himself at another's expense **[154]** without just cause, which is contrary to the law of God and of nature. More equitable is a decree of the Parlement that the prince can waive his own interest in favor of a convicted defendant, but not the civil interest of another party; going even further, the court gave priority to the civil party over the public treasury with respect to the [money] fine.‡

In another decree handed down on 15 July 1351, it was held that the king could set aside civil law [for his personal convenience] pro-

* The civilians cited in the course of this discussion are Bartolus de Saxoferrato, Angelus de Ubaldis (Angelus de Perusio), Baldus de Ubaldis, Paulus de Castro (Castrensis), and Philippus Decius.

† The paragraph up to here is a bit clearer in L100, A10–C2: "These considerations make it clear that the canon lawyers blunder and go astray in holding that a prince is not bound to his contracts by anything other than a natural obligation, on the ground that [strict] obligation is exclusively of civil law. But this is an error that ought to be eradicated. For who can doubt that the obligation and the contract are of the same nature? Therefore, if contracts are natural, and common to all peoples, it follows that obligations and actions are of the same nature. And there is hardly any contract or obligation that can be thought of which does not belong to the law of nature and the common law of peoples. But suppose we concede that there are some contracts which are founded on the civil law of the particular commonwealth. Will anyone dare deny that the prince is more strictly bound by civil contracts and stipulations than private persons are – so much obliged, indeed, that he cannot impair them even by his supreme authority?"

The canonists are thus represented as contending that although a promise is generally binding by natural law, the obligation to observe it strictly is from civil law, so that a prince, being above the civil law, is not strictly bound and on that account would not be even morally subject to a legal action brought before a civil court. Bodin, claiming to follow the civilians, answers first that the (strict) obligation is also from the law of nature, and second that even if promises and the obligation to enforce them are from civil law, the prince is nonetheless strictly bound. On this latter point, however, Bodin is presumably contending not that the prince is bound by civil law, but rather that having made a contract in accordance with civil law, he is bound by the law of nature to keep it strictly.

‡ "... going even further ... fine." L100, D2–3 is clearer: "and that the rights of creditors are to come before penalties paid to the public treasury."

vided it was without prejudice to the rights of private persons, which corroborates the positions we have taken on absolute power. Thus King Philip [VI] of Valois, in two testaments that he made in 1347 and 1350 (which are in the treasury of France, in a chest with the inscrip-
93} tion "testaments of the kings," number 289) appended a clause setting aside customs and civil laws as though they did not bind him; and he did the same in a gift given to the queen on 21 November 1330 (which may be found in Register 66, letter 837). But in a similar situation, the emperor Augustus, wishing to give his wife, Livia, more than was permitted by the *lex Voconia*,[53] asked for a dispensation from the Senate (even though he did not need to, having long since been exempted from the civil law), the better to assure his gift since, as we have said, he was not a sovereign prince.* If he had been sovereign, he would not have been bound in any way. Thus it was held in the strongest terms in an opinion of the Parlement {in 1282} that the king was not bound by the customary law of *retraict lignager*[54] when an attempt was made to repurchase the country of Guyne from him, although there are many who maintain the opposite.†

This is why King Philip the Fair, when he established the Parlements of Paris and Montpellier, declared that they would not be
94} bound by Roman law. And at the founding of universities, our kings have always declared that they would accept the teaching of civil and canon law to be used only at their discretion, without their being bound to it in any way. And for the same reason Alaric, king of the Goths, made it a capital offense to adduce Roman law against his ordinances, which Charles Du Moulin, took ill and **[155]** called barbaric.[55] But he [Alaric] did something that any sovereign prince might do, and rightly ought to do.‡ In like manner, Charles the Fair of

*For "But in a similar situation ... not a sovereign prince" L100, D12–L101, A3 substitutes and explains, "But the emperor Augustus did not think that he could do the same in his commonwealth because, as I have already told you, he did not have the rights of sovereignty. For even though he had been exempted from all the rest of his country's laws, he was not able to make law for his own case. Hence, wishing to give a present to his wife, Livia, he petitioned the Senate for dispensation from the *lex Voconia*, which he would not have needed to do if he had possession of the rights of sovereignty (*si iura maiestatis haberet*)."

†L101, A8–10 elaborates, "because they consider that rule a part of the common law of peoples, and not peculiar to a single commonwealth, although it seemed to the Romans that no law was more unfair."

‡L101, B11–C2 adds, "For subjects will remember and hope for the government of foreigners as long as they use their laws."

this kingdom forbade the citation of Roman law against our customs. This was also the purpose of an ancient decree that I have read in the records of the Parlement by which advocates, in three words as it were, are expressly forbidden to do that: "Let advocates not make so bold as to set written [Roman] law against our custom."

Oldrado, too, writes that the kings of Spain decreed that no one, on pain of death, should plead the Roman law. This prohibition means that judges neither can nor ought to be constrained to judge according to Roman law, even where custom and ordinance are not in conflict with it, much less the prince who dispenses judges from it and
{395} leaves its use to their discretion.* Indeed, it is treason to pose Roman law against the ordinance of one's prince. And because this had become the practice in Spain, King Stephen of Spain, writes Policraticus [John of Salisbury], prohibited the study of Roman law there;[56] and by another ordinance, this one by Alphonso X, all magistrates were required to have recourse to the king[57] when there was no [applicable] ordinance or custom.

Baldus is mistaken when he writes that the French use Roman law only in so far as it is reasonable (*pour raison seulement*), but the Italians are strictly bound by it. The one is bound as little as the other, even though Italy, Spain, and the regions of Provence, Savoy, Languedoc, and Lyon make more use of Roman law than other peoples. And although the emperor Frederick Barbarossa caused the texts of Roman law to be published, the largest part of it is not applied in Italy, and even less of it in Germany. For there is a great difference between right (*droit*) and law (*loy*). Right is based on pure equity; law implies command. For the law is nothing but the command of a sovereign making use of his power. Hence just as a sovereign prince is not bound to the laws of the Greeks or of any foreigner whatever, so
{396} also with the Roman laws, to which he is bound even less than to his own, except in so far as they conform to natural law, to which law, says Pindar, all kings and princes are subject.[58]

And we must not except the pope or the emperor **[156]**, the way

*For "Oldrado too . . . to their discretion" L101, C4–10 substitutes, "Indeed, the kings of Spain, as Oldrado reports, made it a captial offense to appeal to Roman law even in confirmation of their own. Even where there was nothing in their country's laws and customs that differed from Roman law, the effect of their prohibition was to let everybody know that their judges were not bound by Roman law in deciding the cases of their citizens, and much less the prince himself, who judged pernicious any obligation on the part of judges that bound them to a foreign law."

some flatterers do who say that these two can seize the goods of their subjects without cause. Although many doctors, and even many canonists, detest that opinion as contrary to the law of God, they very wrongly limit it by saying that those authorities can do it by invoking
97} their absolute authority.* It would be better to say by force of arms, which is the right of the stronger and of thieves, seeing that absolute power extends only to setting civil law aside, as we have shown above, and that it cannot do violence to the law of God, who has loudly and clearly told us by His law that it is illicit to take, or even to covet, another person's goods. Indeed, those who uphold such opinions are even more dangerous than those who carry them out. They show the lion his claws and arm princes with a show of justice; then the tyrant's wickedness, fed by these opinions, takes flight with power unrestrained and urges on his violent passions, turning avarice into confiscation, love into adultery, and anger into murder. Just as the thunder comes before the lightning, even though in appearance it is just the opposite, so the bad prince, once depraved by pernicious doctrines, makes the fine precede the accusation and the condemnation precede the proof.

It is a kind of legal absurdity to say that it is in the power of the prince to act dishonestly, since his power should always be measured
98} by the standard of justice. Thus Pliny the Younger said to the emperor Trajan: *Ut enim foelicitatis est posse quantum velis, sic magnitudinis velle quantum possis*, which means that the highest degree of happiness is to be able to do what you want, and of greatness to want to do what you can, and shows that a prince can do nothing unjust. It is also a mistake to say that a sovereign prince has power to steal another's goods and to do evil, since it is rather impotence, weakness, and cowardice.

If the prince, then, does not have power to overstep the bounds of natural law, which has been established by God, of whom he is the image, he will also not be able to take another's property without just and reasonable cause [157] – as by purchase, exchange, lawful confiscation,† or in negotiating terms of peace with an enemy, if it cannot otherwise be concluded than by taking the property of private individuals for the preservation of the state.[59] Many [commentators]

*L102, B1–2 attributes this opinion only to canonists speaking of the pope.
†L102, D13–L103, A1 adds, "or in concluding an alliance with friends."

are not of this opinion.* But natural reason would have the public [interest] preferred over the private, and have subjects not only pass over their injuries and desires for revenge, but give up their possessions also for the welfare of the commonwealth, as is ordinarily done
{399} by one public toward another public, and by one individual toward another.†

Thus the Treaty of Peronne, concluded to deliver King Louis XI from imprisonment by the count of Charolais, states that the lord of Torcy would {not} be able to enforce a decree he had obtained against the lord of Saveuse. And Thrasibulus was praised for declaring a general amnesty for all losses and injuries suffered among private parties after he had expelled the thirty tyrants of Athens, which was also done later on at Rome on the occasion of the treaty concluded between the partisans of Caesar on the one side, and the conspirators on the other. Nevertheless, one should try as much as possible to recompense the loss of some with the profit of others, and if this cannot be done without causing trouble, one should take the money from the public treasury, or else borrow it. Thus Aratus [of Sicyon] borrowed sixty thousand crowns to help reimburse those who had been banished and driven from properties that had then become the property of others through prescription of long time.

In the absence of the causes I have mentioned, the prince can neither take nor dispose of another's property without the consent of its owner. And in all the gifts, favors, privileges, and acts of the prince,
{400} the clause "saving the rights of others"‡ is always implied, even if not

* For "not of this opinion" L103, A4–7 substitutes, "although some hold that each should have his own, that private possessions cannot be impaired by the public or, if public necessity demands it, that the individual should be compensated by all collectively – which is an opinion that I endorse if it can be done conveniently."

† "... as is ordinarily done ... toward another." This clause seems to deal directly with the duty to abandon public and private claims in order to have peace. L103, B1–7 elaborates at length: "For in a [treaty] of peace there is almost always something unjust for which the welfare of the public is the recompense. And it is a rule of justice practiced by every people that in making peace not only are public losses to be borne by the public and private losses by individuals, but each must compensate the other through their gains and losses. I am aware that many experts of both [civil and canon] law have been, and are, of the opinion that, in treaties containing a clause to the effect that losses incurred on either side shall not be questioned, the exception is void and does not prejudice the rights of private parties. But we follow a different rule."

‡ For "saving the rights of others" L103, D12–13 substitutes, "Be it done without harm to me or any other (*Quod sine mea, aut alterius fraude fiat*)," on which L103, n. 27 comments, "In the vernacular it reads, 'Fully reserving our own and others' rights (*Sauf en tout nostre droit et l'autrui*).' "

expressed. In fact, the inclusion of this clause by the emperor Maximilian in the investiture of King Louis XII with the duchy of Milan was the occasion for a new war by the Sforzas to preserve their legal claim to that duchy, which the emperor had neither the right nor the wish to give away.* For the saying that princes are the lords (*seigneurs*) of everything applies only to legitimate governance and supreme judicial power (*droite seigneurie et justice souveraine*), leaving to each the possession and property of his goods. As Seneca said, *Ad reges potestas omnium pertinet, ad singulos proprietas*,† and a little further on, *Omnia Rex imperio possidet, singuli dominio*.‡

For this reason [158] our kings are required by the ordinances and decrees of the court [Parlement] to rid their hands of properties that have fallen to them by right of confiscation or by escheat of a foreigner's estate (*par droit de confiscation ou d'aubeine*), unless it was held directly and immediately of the crown, so that the mesne lords [of these properties] may lose nothing of their rights.§ Furthermore, if the king is his subject's debtor, he is liable to judgment. And so that foreigners and posterity may know how sincerely our kings have accepted legal proceedings, let me cite a verdict from the year 1419 which dismissed letters of restitution[60] that the king had obtained to
01} cover judgments in default which had been secured against him.[61] By another verdict handed down in 1266, the king was condemned to pay his curate a tenth of the fruits of his garden. Private parties are not treated that strictly, and the sovereign prince is never reinstated in his rights by virtue of being a minor, but is always reputed to be of age when it is a matter of his private interest.¶ The commonwealth,

*For "by the Sforzas . . . give away" L104, A4–5 substitutes, "for the Sforza family, relying on these words, contended that the entire right to that principality had been left with them by the emperor."

†"To kings belongs the power over everything, to private individuals the property."

‡"The king possesses everything in governance, individuals in ownership."

§For "For this reason . . . their rights" L104, B1–4 substitutes, "This is the reason why our kings are compelled to grant to private persons, or otherwise to dispose of the infeudated lands (*praedia fiduciarum*) of [sub]vassals that have been assigned to the treasury by right of confiscation. This is done so that the prince's vassals and the mesne lords of those who suffered confiscation may continue to enjoy their rights." The point here seems to be that the mesne lords of properties escheated to the treasury must be able to assert their rights in those properties, which they can do only if the prince grants or sells them to private parties who will therewith assume the obligations that attached to them.

¶L104, C8–9 adds, "For the benefit of the commonwealth, the Roman emperors (*principes*) used to be reinstated, but we follow a different rule."

however, is always considered to be a minor, and the answer to those who hold that the state ought never to be granted reinstatement is that they are confusing the [private] patrimony of the prince with the public treasure. These are always kept separate in a monarchy, although they are all one in democratic and aristocratic states.*

Thus do we see the rectitude of our kings and the equity of our Parlements, who have given preference to the commonwealth over private individuals, and to private individuals over kings. There still exists a verdict of the Parlement delivered against King Charles VII, by which he was condemned to have the woods that he owned near the city of Paris cut down for public and private use; and the price was even fixed in the decree, which is something that would not be done to a private party. Then could one see at a glance the difference between a true prince and a tyrant. For although Charles VII was a great king and victorious over all his enemies, when it came to reason, equity, and the judgment of his magistrates, he was more yielding and
{402} more pliant than the lowest of his subjects. Yet at that very time, Philip Maria, the duke of Milan, prohibited the passage and crossing of his rivers, and any use thereof, without his leave, which he sold for money.

Up to now we have spoken of the way in which the prince is subject to the laws and to contracts entered into by him **[159]** with his subjects. It remains to be seen whether he is subject to the contracts of his predecessors, and if that obligation is compatible with sovereignty. Briefly to resolve an infinity of questions that can be raised on this siubject, I hold that if the kingdom is hereditary, the prince is fully bound [to the contracts of his predecessor], just as a private heir would be according to the rules of [private] law. The same holds if the kingdom is transferred by testament to someone other than the next in line, as by Ptolemy, king of Cyrene; Nicomedes, king of Bithynia; Attalus, king of Asia; and Eumenes, king of Pergamum,[62] in making the Roman people the heir of their kingdoms, states, and principalities. But a kingdom may be passed by testament to the next in line, as the kingdom of England was passed by the testament of
{403} King Henry VIII to Edward VI, for whom his sister, Mary, was the substitute, and, for Mary, Elizabeth, each of whom enjoyed posses-

*For "confusing the [private] patrimony . . . aristocratic states" L104, D1–2 substitutes, "confusing the cause (*causa*) of the prince and the commonwealth, which is considered to be legally the same in democratic states, but not in the other forms."

sion of the state in turn. In this case we must distinguish whether the heir by designation wishes to accept the kingdom in that capacity, or prefers to renounce the succession as the beneficiary of a testament and to claim the crown in virtue of the custom and law of the land [dealing with succession to the throne]. In the first case, the successor is bound by the acts and promises of his predecessor, just as a private heir would be. But in the second case, he is not bound by the acts of his predecessor even if he [the predecessor] swore to that effect. For the oath of a predecessor does not bind a successor [of the second sort], although the successor is bound by an act that turns out to be of profit to the kingdom.[63]

This is why King Louis XII, when asked to return artillery that had been loaned to Charles VIII, replied that he was not that ruler's heir. I have also seen and read letters of more recent memory by King Francis II, who writes to the rulers of the [Swiss] leagues on 19 January 1559 as follows:

> Even though we are not bound to pay the debts contracted by our greatly honored late lord and father, inasmuch as we have not come into possession of this crown as his heir, but by the law and custom generally observed in this kingdom since its beginning, which law obligates us to observe only those treaties made and acknowledged by the kings our predecessors with other princes and republics for the welfare and advantage of this crown; nevertheless, wishing to keep the pledge (*descharger la conscience*) of our late lord and father, we **[160]** have resolved to discharge those that shall be found honestly due, etc., while asking you to reduce the interest charges to the rate that is current in your country and permitted by your laws.

04} This was accepted by the Swiss, and the interest which they had been taking at sixteen percent was reduced to five percent, all of which was in accord with an ancient decision given in the year 1256, by which it was held that the king was not obligated by the debts of his predecessors.

Hence it is a mistake to stop at the literal meaning of the words used in this regard at the coronation of the kings of France. After the archbishop of Reims has placed the crown on the king's head, the twelve peers of France extend their hands towards him, and address him thus:

> Stay here and henceforth enjoy [possession of] the state. Up to

> now you have held it by right of succession from your father (*par succession paternelle*) and now it is put into your hands, as the true heir, by God almighty and by the delivery that we, the bishops and other servants of God,* now make to you.

For it is beyond doubt that the king never dies, as they say, and that as soon as one is deceased the nearest male of his stock is seized of the
{405} kingdom and in possession thereof before he is crowned. It is not passed by right of succession from the father (*par succession paternelle*) but rather in virtue of the kingdom's law.†

If a sovereign prince has made a contract in his capacity as sovereign on a matter that concerns the state and brings it profit, the successors are bound by it. And much more are they bound if the agreement was made with the consent of the Estates, or the principal towns and communities, or the Parlements, or the princes and greatest nobles. Given the pledge of faith and obligation by the kingdom's subjects, the successors would be bound even if the agreement was disadvantageous to the public. But if the prince had contracted with a foreigner, or even with a subject, on some matter of interest to the public, without the consent of those whom I have mentioned, then if the contract is highly prejudicial to the public, his {public law} successor in the state is not bound in any way, and all the less so if he succeeds by right of election. In that case, one cannot say that he holds anything from his predecessor, as he would if he had the state by way of conferment (*resignation*).[64] But if the acts of his predecessors have turned to the profit of the public, the successor is always bound

*For "the bishops and other servants of God" L106, A5 substitutes, "from us, the bishops and peers."

†"For it is beyond doubt . . . kingdom's law." L106, A5–B6 substitutes and clarifies in order to deny any suggestion of a power of election in the coronation ceremony as just quoted, "An honest speech, if only it were true. For there can be no doubt, in my opinion, that the king comes into possession of authority and of the title thereto (*ac proprietate*) before he is consecrated, and that this is not by hereditary right or right of succession from his father (*non quidem haereditario aut paterno iure*), and even less by favor (*beneficio*) of the bishops or the peers, but by the law of succession to the kingship (*lege regia*). This principle was registered long ago [1468] in a decree of the French Senate [the Parlement of Paris], so that no one should think that royal power depends on the choice of the bishops. It was [set down] not because the Senate [Parlement] doubted that royal power was in being before the inauguration, but to dispel the bishops' empty casuistries. We have been taught by that old and time-worn proverb of our ancestors that with us the king never dies, so that everyone may understand that, when a prince dies, authority and power are transferred in that very instant to the next in line lest there be any uncertainty in the succession to the throne, which is the worst plague that can happen in a commonwealth."

by them, no matter in what capacity he holds [the throne]. Otherwise, **[161]** he would be permitted to derive profit from another's loss by fraud and deviousness, against equity and natural reason, and the commonwealth could perish in its time of need because no one would be willing to give it aid.

Accordingly, the decisions of the Parlement, given in 1256 and
06} 1294 and recorded in the book entitled *Olim*,[65] in which it was stated that the king [of France] would not be bound by the obligations of his predecessor, have been confirmed by many other decisions given in like cases, as I have said. Thus the opinion of Baldus has been disproved; without making the distinctions we have laid down, he would have a sovereign prince removed from power if he did not execute the testament of his predecessor.

But why must we introduce distinctions, someone will object, since all princes are obliged to honor the common law of peoples, and contracts and testaments are founded on it?* I reply that these distinctions are necessary because a prince is not obligated by the common law of peoples any more than by his own edicts, and if the common law of peoples is unjust, the prince can depart from it in edicts made for his kingdom and forbid his subjects to use it. That is the way the law of slavery was handled in this kingdom, even though it was common to all† peoples. And this can also be done in other matters of a similar nature provided that the result is not contrary to the law of God. For if justice is the end of law, law the work of the prince, and the prince the image of God; then by this reasoning, the law of the prince must be modelled on the law of God.

*L106, D11–13 adds, "This would not be true if we considered the entire range [of wills and contracts]. But even if we concede the point . . ."

†For "all" L107, A5 substitutes, "almost all."

BOOK I, CHAPTER 10
On the true marks of sovereignty*

[211] Since there is nothing greater on earth, after God, than sovereign princes, and since they have been established by Him as His lieutenants for commanding other men, we need to be precise about their status (*qualité*) so that we may respect and revere their majesty in complete [212] obedience, and do them honor in our thoughts and in our speech. Contempt for one's sovereign prince is contempt toward God, of whom he is the earthly image. That is why God, speaking to Samuel, from whom the people had demanded a
{478} different prince, said "It is me that they have wronged."

To be able to recognize such a person – that is, a sovereign – we have to know his attributes (*marques*, *nota*), which are properties not shared by subjects. For if they were shared, there would be no sovereign prince. Yet the best writers on this subject have not treated this point with the clarity it deserves, whether from flattery, fear, hatred, or forgetfulness.

We read that Samuel, after consecrating the king that God had designated, wrote a book about the rights of majesty. But the Hebrews have written that the kings suppressed his book so that they could tyrannize their subjects. Melanchthon thus went astray in thinking that the rights of majesty were the abuses and tyrannical practices that Samuel pointed out to the people in a speech.[1] "Do you

* The French speaks of marks (*marques*) of sovereignty as though the problem was to show the ordinary subject how to discern which of the many authorities placed over him was entitled to ultimate obedience. But since the distinctive marks of a sovereign in Bodin's account are a state of juridical prerogatives (and not force or ceremonial honors *per se*), the idea perhaps is better expressed by the Latin (147, C2) *iura* (rights or prerogatives).

wish to know," said Samuel, "the ways of tyrants?* It is to seize the goods of subjects to dispose of at his pleasure, and to seize their women and their children in order to abuse them and to make them slaves." The word *mishpotim* [Hebrew] as it is used in this passage does not mean rights, but rather practices and ways of doing things. Otherwise this good prince, Samuel, would have contradicted himself. For when accounting to the people for the stewardship that God
79} had given him, he said, "Is there anyone among you who can say that I ever took gold or silver from him, or any present whatsoever?" And thereupon the whole people loudly praised him for never having done a wrong or taken anything from anyone no matter who.

Among the best known Greek writers, there is not one who has written anything on this subject except for Aristotle, Polybius, and Dionysius of Halicarnassus. But they have been so brief that one can see at a glance that they offer no clear resolution of this question. I will repeat the words of Aristotle. "There are," he says, "three parts of a state, one in deliberating and taking counsel; another in creating officers and establishing the duties of each; and the third in rendering justice."[2] Even though he says "parts of the state," we must take him to be speaking of the rights of sovereignty, unless we are to admit that he never spoke of sovereignty at all, for there is only **[213]** this passage. Polybius too fails to define the rights and marks of sovereignty. But he does say, speaking of the Romans, that their state was a mixture of royal power, aristocratic lordship, and popular liberty, because the people makes the laws and elects the officers; the Senate makes arrangements for the provinces, administers the finances, receives ambassadors, and deals with all the highest matters; and the consuls have a prerogative of honor that is royal in form and dignity, especially in wartime when they are all-powerful.† It thus appears that he touched on all the principal points of sovereignty since he is saying that those who hold them have sovereignty. But on this subject Dionysius of Halicarnassus seems to have written better and more clearly than all the others. For he says that King Servius, wishing to strip the Senate of its power, gave the people the power to

*For "tyrants" L147, D7 substitutes "princes," which makes much better sense.

†Bodin refers generally to *Histories*, Book VI. L148, C1 adds that the consuls have the power "to convene the Senate and the people and to conduct warfare (*bellum . . . gerere*) at their own discretion."

make and repeal laws, to declare war and make peace, to appoint and
{480} remove officers, and to take appeals from all the magistrates. In another place, speaking of the third conflict at Rome between the nobility and the people, he says that the consul M. Valerius told the people that it ought to be content with having the power of making laws, appointing officers, and hearing cases as the court of last resort, and that the rest belonged to the Senate.*

Subsequently, the jurists expanded this list of rights (the modern[3] much more than the ancient) in treatises which they call "Regalian Rights," and which they have filled with an infinity of minutiae that are shared by dukes, counts, barons, bishops, officers, and other subjects of sovereign princes.† This results in their using the term "sovereign prince" for dukes like those of Milan, Mantua, Ferrara, and Savoy, and indeed even for various counts. All of them have made this error, which is, no doubt, very easily mistaken for the truth. For who would not deem someone sovereign who gives law to all his subjects, makes peace and declares war, provides (*pourvoit*)[4] all the officers and magistrates of the land, levies taxes and exempts whom he pleases, and pardons persons who deserve to die? What more could one desire in a sovereign prince?

Such persons thus have all the indicia (*marques*) of sovereignty, and yet we have shown above‡ that the dukes of Milan, Savoy, Ferrara, Florence, and Mantua hold **[214]** of the Empire, and that the most
{481} honorable titles they can take are those of princes and vicars of the Empire. We have shown that they receive their investiture from the Empire and that they render fealty and homage to it – in short, that they are natural subjects of the Empire, being natives of lands subject to it. How then could they be sovereign absolutely? How indeed can someone be sovereign who recognizes the jurisdiction (*justice*) of someone greater than himself – of someone who quashes his verdicts and corrects his laws, and punishes him if he behaves abusively? We have shown that Galeazzo I, the viscount of Milan, was accused of

*L148, C11 adds, "He thus appears to have touched on the chief heads of sovereignty."

†For "Subsequently the jurists expanded . . . sovereign princes" L148, C11–D3 substitutes, "This appears to have touched upon the chief heads of sovereignty which modern jurists, in their rambling disputations, have confused with the duties of magistrates and made into powers shared with dukes, counts, bishops, and provincial governors." The French thus objects to the triviality of the minor rights taken up in these treatises, the Latin to confusion about the central rights of sovereignty. The latter seems more appropriate in context.

‡In Book I, chapter 9 (not translated).

treason, found guilty in fact and law, and condemned by the emperor for having levied taxes (*tailles*) on his subjects without permission, and died in prison. And if some by permission, others by sufferance, and still others by usurpation, do things that go beyond the power they were given, does it follow that they are sovereigns, seeing that they themselves admit that they are vicars and princes of the Empire?[5] They would rather have to cast out these titles as well as the title of duke and the rank of "highness," and, calling themselves kings, employ the title of "majesty," which cannot be done without disavowing the Empire, as did Galvagno, viscount of Milan, who was severely punished for it. We have also shown that, by the treaty of Constance [1183], the cities of Lombardy remained subject to the Empire. In short, we have shown what intolerable absurdities would follow if vassals were sovereigns, especially when they have nothing that is not held of someone else. For this is to equate the lord and the subject, the master and the servant, him who gives the law and him who receives it, him who commands and him who owes obedience.

Since this is impossible, we have to conclude that dukes, counts,
32} and all of those who hold of another or receive laws or commands from another, whether by force or legal obligation, are not sovereign. And we will say the same of the highest magistrates, lieutenant-generals of kings, governors, regents, dictators. No matter how much power they have, if they are bound to the laws, jurisdiction, and command of someone else, they are not sovereign. For the prerogatives of sovereignty have to be of such a sort that they apply only to a sovereign prince. If, on the contrary, **[215]** they can be shared with subjects, one cannot say that they are marks of sovereignty. For just as a crown no longer has that name if it is breached, or if its rosettes are torn away, so sovereign majesty loses its greatness if someone makes a breach in it and encroaches on a part of its domain. This is why, in the exchange of the lands of Mantes and Meulan for Montpellier between King Charles V and the king of Navarre, the rights of the crown (*droits Royaux*) are articulated [in the contract] and are said to belong to the king in their entirety, and to him alone.

By the same reasoning all {the jurists} agree that the rights of the crown (*droits Royaux*) cannot be relinquished or alienated, and cannot
33} be prescribed by any period of time.* And if it should happen that a

*L149, D6–7 adds, "which is why Baldus calls them the holy of holies (*sacra sacrorum*) and Cyno [da Pistoia] inseparable entities (*individua*)." For an extended list of legal

sovereign prince does share them with a subject, he would make a companion of his servant and, in so doing, would cease to be sovereign. For the notion of a sovereign (that is to say, of someone who is above all subjects) cannot apply to someone who has made a subject his companion. Just as God, the great sovereign, cannot make a God equal to Himself because He is infinite and by logical necessity (*par demonstration necessaire*) two infinites cannot exist, so we can say that the prince, whom we have taken as the image of God, cannot make a subject equal to himself without annihilation of his power.

This being so, it follows that the [distinctive] mark of sovereignty is not to do justice, because that is shared by prince and subject, nor is it to establish or remove all officers, because both the prince and subject have that power too. This applies not only to officers serving in the administration of justice, police, war, or finance, but also to those who have command in peace or war. For we read that the consuls in the early days of the Republic appointed military tribunes who were like marshals in the army, and that the person whom they called the *interrex* appointed the dictator[6] while the dictator appointed the
{*484*} master of the horse. And in every state where the administration of justice goes with fiefs, the feudal lord appoints officers and can remove them without cause unless they have received their offices by way of compensation. Our verdict is the same as to the rewards and punishments that magistrates and captains, quite as much as a sovereign prince, give to those who have earned or incurred them. Giving rewards or punishments **[216]** according to desert is not a mark of sovereignty since it is common to the prince and to the magistrate, even though the magistrate has this power from the prince. Taking counsel on affairs of state is also not a mark of sovereignty. It is properly the task of the privy council, or senate, of the commonwealth, which is always kept distinct from the sovereign, especially in a democracy, where sovereignty resides in the assembly of the people. Far from being appropriate for the people,* deliberation on affairs ought not to be allowed to it at all, as we shall explain in due course.

We can thus conclude that not one of the three points laid down by Aristotle is a distinctive mark of sovereignty. And as for what Dio-

commentaries cited by Bodin on the inalienability of sovereignty, see IP, p. 482, n.a. and n. 15.

*L150, B7 adds, "which is always the enemy of good counsel and prudence."

nysius of Halicarnassus said – namely, that M. Valerius, in the speech he made to the Roman people to calm their discontents, argued that the people ought to be content with the power to make the laws and create the magistrates – that does not go far enough to make us understand what the rights of sovereignty are, as I have pointed out above in discussing the creation of magistrates. For we would say the same of the laws that a magistrate can give to persons within his jurisdiction, provided that he does nothing contrary to the edicts and
35} ordinances of his sovereign prince. To clarify this point, we must assume that the term "law," used without qualification, signifies the just command of the person or persons who have full power over everyone else without excepting anybody, and no matter whether the command affects subjects collectively or as individuals, and excepting only the person or persons who made the law.*

To speak more strictly, law is the command of the sovereign affecting all the subjects in general, or dealing with general interests, as Festus Pompeius said, whereas privilege is directed to a few individuals. If it [the measure] is from the privy council, or senate, of a commonwealth, it is called a *senatusconsultum* – a decree of the privy council or ordinance of the Senate. If the common people at Rome {*plebs*} issued a command, they called it a *plebiscitum*, or command of the commoners, although it was ultimately called a law after a number of struggles between the commoners and the nobility. In order to settle these conflicts, the entire people, meeting in the *comitia centuriata* (*l'assemblee des grands estats*),[7] passed a law at the request of M. Horatius, the consul, that the nobility and the Senate as a whole, and each one of the people taken individually **[217]**, should be bound to keep the ordinances of the commoners without appeal and without permitting the nobility to have a voice. And since the nobility and the Senate paid no attention to this, the same law was renewed and published again and yet again at the request of Quintus Hortensius

*"And as for what Dionysius of Halicarnassus said . . . person or persons who made the law." L150, B9–C8 is somewhat clearer: "And as for what Dionysius of Halicarnassus wrote of the consul, M. Valerius, [who said] that the power of making laws and creating magistrates was in the people – even that, as we have said, is not enough for identifying the rights of sovereignty. For the power of making law is not truly sovereign unless we mean the prince's law, since magistrates also have laws of their own, which they can make for persons within their jurisdiction so long as they contain nothing in conflict with the prince's laws. To make this even clearer, let us define laws in the strict sense as the just commands of the sovereign power, whether it be in the hands of one, of all, or of a few."

and Publilius Philo, both dictators, and from then on, they no longer said *plebiscitum*, or ordinance of the common people, but used the term "law" without qualification for any of the commoners' commands.[8] Whether the scope was public or particular, or whether the
{486} commoners were convened to appoint judges or themselves to judge, what they did was spoken of as law.

As for commands of magistrates, they are not called laws, but edicts only. *Est enim edictum iussum magistratus*,* says Varro. These bind only those who are within his jurisdiction, provided that the commands do not conflict with the ordinances of higher magistrates or with the laws and commands of the sovereign prince.† These commands, moreover, remain in force only as long as the magistrate continues in office, and since all magistracies were annual in the Roman Republic, edicts were valid for a year at most.‡ This is why Cicero, indicting Verres, said, *qui plurimum edicto tribuunt, legem annuam appellant, tu plus edicto complecteris quam lege*.§ And because the emperor Augustus styled himself only *imperator*, or commander-in-chief, and tribune of the people, he called his own ordinances edicts, but those made by the people at his request were called *leges Iuliae*.[9] Since other emperors adopted this way of speaking, the word edict was gradually taken to mean law when it came from the mouth of the person who had sovereign power, no matter whether it was for everyone or a single individual, or whether the edict was continuing or temporary. It is thus an abuse of words to call a law an edict. However this may be, it is only sovereign princes who can make law for all subjects without exception, both collectively and individually.

Objection will be made that the Roman Senate had power to make law and that most of the great affairs of state, in peace as well as war, were in its hands. We shall speak later on of the power of the senate,
{487} or privy council, of a commonwealth¶ [218] – as it ought to be and as it was at Rome. But to reply in passing to the objection I have mentioned, I say that the Roman Senate, from the expulsion of the

*"An edict is the command of a magistrate."
†L151, A1 adds, "or Senate decrees."
‡L151, A5–8 adds, "And so successors in a given office were expected to approve or disapprove previous edicts, and if there was anything in conflict with the laws or beyond the jurisdiction of the incumbent who had ordered it, it was not ratified."
§"Those who attribute the most to an edict call it a law lasting for a year, but with you an edict goes even further than a law."
¶Book III, chapter 1 (not translated here).

kings up to the emperors,* never had the power to make law, but merely certain ordinances that were valid only for a year and did not bind the assembly of the commoners, much less the assembly of the entire people. Many commentators are mistaken on this point, including even Conan, who says that the senate had the power to make permanent laws. For Dionysius of Halicarnassus, who had diligently studied the commentaries of Marcus Varro, wrote that decrees of the Senate had no force at all if the people did not authorize them, and that even if they were authorized, they were valid only for a year unless they were published in the form of a law. Nor was it any different at Athens, where decrees of the senate were [also] annual, as Demosthenes says in his speech against Aristocrates. And if it was an affair of great consequence, they brought it to the people to dispose of as it saw fit, which led {the philosopher} Anarchasis to observe that "at Athens the wise propose, and fools dispose."

Thus the Senate only deliberated; the people gave commands – as one can see in Livy, who so often uses the formula *Senatus decrevit, populus iussit*.† This holds even though the magistrates, and even the tribunes, usually accepted what the Senate did on sufferance if it did not strike at the power of the common people {*plebis*} or the sovereignty of the Estates {*populi*}. The ancient Romans put it clearly when they said *Imperium in magistratibus, auctoritatem in Senatu, potestatem*[10] *in plebe, maiestatem in populo*.‡ For the term "majesty" is
88} appropriate only for the person whose hand is on the rudder of sovereignty.

Although the *lex Iulia de maiestate*, made by the people at the request of the Emperor Augustus, held that anyone who struck a magistrate while performing the duties of his office was guilty of *lèse majesté*, and although in Latin histories, and even in the jurists, one constantly encounters phrases such as *maiestatem Consulis, maiestatem Praetoris*,§ this is nevertheless an improper way of speaking. In our [French] laws and ordinances, the crime of *lèse majesté* does not apply to dukes, princes, or magistrates of any sort, but only to the sovereign

*For "up to the emperors" L151, C4–5 substitutes, "up to the dominate of Tiberius Caesar." (At one point, Tiberius did in fact make a show of enhancing the force of Senate decrees.)

†"The Senate decreed, the people ordered."

‡"Command [is] in the magistrates, authority in the Senate, power in the commons, and sovereignty in the people."

§"The majesty of the Consul, the majesty of the Praetor."

prince. And the ordinance of King Sigismund **[219]** of Poland, issued in 1538, states that the crime of *lèse majesté* will not apply beyond his person, which is in accord with the true and proper signification of the term *lèse majesté*. This is also the reason, it seems, why the dukes of Saxony, Bavaria, Savoy, Lorraine, Ferrara, and Mantua do not include the term "majesty" among their titles, but rather "highness," and the duke of Venice, "serenity."

This last, by the way, is a prince {*princeps*} properly so called, which is to say "the first." For he is nothing but the first among the gentlemen of Venice, and has no more than the privilege of speaking last when decisions are made in any council at which he is present. And just as at Rome the edicts of magistrates obligated every private individual provided that they did not conflict with Senate decrees; and decrees of the Senate did not bind the magistrates if contrary to the ordinances of the commoners; and ordinances of the commoners were above decrees of the Senate; and a law of the assembly of all the people was above everything – so at Venice the ordinances of magistrates obligate private individuals according to the scope and jurisdiction of each magistrate, but the corporation or college of the
{*489*} Ten is above the individual magistrates, the senate is above the Ten, and the Great Council, which is the assembly of all the gentlemen of Venice above the age of twenty, has sovereignty above the senate, such that, if the Ten are divided,* they appeal to the Council of Sages, which numbers twenty-two, and if these cannot agree, the Senate is assembled, although if the affair involves high prerogatives of sovereignty, they convene the Great Council. Accordingly, when the Ten pass an ordinance, the words *In Consiglio Di Dieci* are used, and if the Sages were present, *Con La Giunta* is added. If the ordinance is by the senate, the formula is *In Pregadi*; if the assembly of Venetian gentlemen, *In Consiglio Maggiore*. All their laws and statutes are made in these three[11] corporations or colleges. But ordinary affairs of state are dealt with by the Seven, which they call the governing body (*segnorie*).†

It is thus by sufferance only that the Ten or the senate make ordinances, and these obtain the force of law only in so far as they are

*For "divided" L152, C4 substitutes, "equally divided."

†For "But ordinary affairs . . . governing body" L152, D24 substitutes, "except for the matters that the Seven (which is the most secret council of the state) have customarily decided on their own."

found just and reasonable, just as the edicts of the ancient Roman praetors, if they were equitable **[220]** and just, were renewed by their successors and over time received as laws, although new praetors were not obligated to keep them and were always empowered to make others. But the jurist Julian decided to collect a goodly number of what he thought were the best of these edicts, and after interpreting and editing them in ninety books, he presented them to the emperor Hadrian as a gift. As a reward, the emperor made him the high prefect of Rome; subsequently his {grand}son became emperor. Hadrian also had these edicts ratified (*homologués*) by the Senate, and added his own authority to give them the force of laws. Nevertheless,
[illegible]0} the name "edict" persisted, and that has led many [jurists] to make the mistake of regarding these edicts as ordinances made by the praetors.* Justinian did pretty much the same with the edicts collected and interpreted by the other jurists, ratifying those he liked and rejecting the rest, the name "edict" still remaining. Yet it is no more an edict than if a sovereign prince should ratify the opinions of Bartolus or the ordinances of his magistrates. That sort of thing has been done many times in this kingdom when our kings, finding various ordinances and decrees of the Parlement especially equitable and just, have ratified them and caused them to be published with the force of laws.

This shows that the power of the law lies in him who has the sovereignty and who gives force to the law through the words, "we have said and have ordained, we do say and ordain, etc.," and who adds the charge at the end with the words, "and so we lay this command upon all etc." This is what the [Roman] emperors expressed when they said *Sancimus* (we enact), which was the word belonging to majesty. Thus the consul Posthumius, in a speech that he delivered to the people, said *Nego iniussu populi quicquam sanciri posse, quod populum teneat.*† Also the magistrate putting a request before the people began with the words, *Quod bonum, faustum, foelixque sit vobis ac reipublicae velitis, iubeatis.*‡ And at the end of the law came the words

*For "these edicts as ordinances made by the praetors" L153, A3 substitutes, "these laws as edicts of the praetor." (The French appears to be superior.)

†"I deny that any enactment can be made without the order of the people that would be binding on the people."

‡"May you wish and may you command what is good, auspicious, and favorable for yourselves and for the commonwealth."

Si quis adversus ea fecerit, etc.,* which was called the *sanctio* (enactment) and contained the rewards and punishments of those who should fulfill or violate the law respectively. **[221]** These are special formulae that went with the majesty of those who had the power to make law, and were not to be found in the edicts of magistrates or in the decrees of the Senate. In addition, the penalty attached to the laws of a sovereign prince is very different from that found in the ordinances of magistrates or of guilds and corporations. These can inflict penalties and fines within certain limits. But only a sovereign prince can attach
{*491*} the death penalty to his edicts,† which was forbidden [to the former] by an ancient decree of the Parlement. The clause on arbitrary punishment affixed to the ordinances of magistrates and governors never goes so far as to include the death penalty.

We may thus conclude that the first prerogative (*marque*) of a sovereign prince is to give law to all in general and each in particular. But this is not sufficient. We have to add "without the consent of any other, whether greater, equal, or below him." For if the prince is obligated to make no law without the consent of a superior, he is clearly a subject; if of an equal, he has an associate; if of subjects, such as the senate or the people, he is not sovereign.† The names of grandees (*seigneurs*) that one finds affixed to edicts are not put there to give the law its force, but to witness it and to add weight to it so that the enactment will be more acceptable. For there are very ancient edicts, extant at Saint Denys in France, issued by Philip I and Louis the Fat in 1060 and 1129 respectively, to which the seals of their queens Anne and Alix [Adelaide of Savoy], and of Robert and Hugh, were affixed. For Louis the Fat, it was year twelve of his reign; for Adelaide, year six.

When I say that the first prerogative of sovereignty is to give law to all in general and to each in particular, the latter part refers to privileges, which are in the jurisdiction of sovereign princes to the
{*492*} exclusion of all others. I call it a privilege when a law is made for one or a few private individuals, no matter whether it is for the profit or the loss of the person with respect to whom it is decreed. Thus Cicero said, *Privilegium de meo capite latum est*. "They have passed," he said, "a capital privilege against me." He is referring to the authorization to

* "If anyone against these shall undertake, etc."

† For "edicts" L153, C2 substitutes, "law."

‡ For "he is not sovereign" L153, C8–9 substitutes, "he has given up supreme authority."

put him on trial decreed against him by the commoners at the request of the tribune Clodius. He calls this the *lex Clodia* in many places, and he bitterly protests that privileges **[222]** could be decreed only by the great Estates of the people {the *comitia centuriata*, that is, the entire people} as it was laid down by the laws of the Twelve Tables in the words: *Privilegia, nisi comitiis centuriatis irroganto, qui secus faxit capital esto.** And all those who have written of regalian rights agree that only the sovereign can grant privileges, exemptions, and immunities, and grant dispensations from edicts and ordinances. In monarchies, however, privileges last only for the lifetime of the monarchs, as the emperor Tiberius, Suetonius reports, informed all those who had received privileges from Augustus.†

{93} Someone may object not only that magistrates have the power of making edicts and ordinances, each within his competence and jurisdiction, but also that private persons make the customs, which can be general as well as local. Custom, surely, has no less power than law, and as the prince is master of the law [it is objected], private persons are masters of the customs. I answer that custom acquires its force little by little and by the common consent of all, or most, over many years, while law appears suddenly, and gets its strength from one person who has the power of commanding all. Custom slips in softly and without violence; law is commanded and promulgated by power, very often against the subjects' wishes; and for that reason Dio Chrysostom compares custom to a king, law to a tyrant. Law, furthermore, can repeal customs, while if custom should detract from law, the magistrate, and those who are charged with making sure the laws are kept, can have the law enforced whenever they see fit. Custom carries neither rewards nor penalties; law always attaches rewards or penalties, unless it is a permissive law that removes the prohibitions of another law. To put it briefly, custom has no force but

*"Let no privileges be imposed except in the *comitia centuriata*; let him who has done otherwise be put to death." L154, A2–3 adds, "Privileges that confer an advantage, however, are more correctly spoken of as benefits (*beneficia*)."

†L154, A6–B1 adds, "If someone should object against me that magistrates often grant exemptions from the law, and that at Rome the Senate did so very frequently, I will answer him with the saying of Papinian: 'We should look not to what is done at Rome but to what ought to be done (*Non quid Romae fiat, sed quid fieri debeat, spectandum esse*).' Yet by the *lex Cornelia tribunitia*, the Roman Senate was forbidden to grant anyone exemption from the laws unless two hundred senators were present, an exception that seems to have been conceded to the Senate because assembling the entire people was so difficult."

by sufferance, and only in so far as it pleases the sovereign prince, who can make it a law by giving it his ratification. Hence the entire force of civil law and custom lies in the power of the sovereign prince.

So much, then, for the first prerogative of sovereignty, which is the power of giving law or issuing commands to all in general and to each
{494} in particular. It cannot be shared with subjects, for even if a sovereign prince [223] should give certain individuals the power to make laws having the same force as if he had made them himself, as did the people of Athens for Solon and the Spartans for Lycurgus, still the laws were not the laws of Solon or of Lycurgus, who were only the commissioners and agents of those who had given them this office, but were the laws of the Athenian and Spartan peoples. In aristocratic and democratic states, a law ordinarily bears the name of the person who has prepared and drafted it, but who is nonetheless a mere agent, the ratification of it belonging to whoever has the sovereignty. Thus we see in Livy that the entire people was assembled to ratify the laws drawn up in twelve tables by the ten commissioners appointed as agents for that purpose.

Also comprised in this power of making and repealing law is its clarification and correction when it is so obscure that the magistrates find it perverse or intolerably absurd for the cases brought before them. The magistrate, however, can bend the law and its interpretation, either to soften or to toughen it, provided that in bending it he takes good care not to break it, even if it seems very harsh. If he does otherwise, the law condemns him to infamy. It is in this sense that we
{495} ought to understand the law called *Laetoria* that Papinian reports without naming its author, which permitted the great praetor* to supplement and correct the laws, for if one understands this otherwise, it would follow that a simple magistrate was above the laws and that he could obligate the people to obey his edicts, which we have shown to be impossible.

This same power of making and repealing law includes all the other rights and prerogatives of sovereignty, so that strictly speaking we can say that there is only this one prerogative of sovereignty, inasmuch as all the other rights are comprehended in it – such as declaring war or making peace; hearing appeals in last instance from the judgments of any magistrate; instituting and removing the highest officers; impos-

*Bodin apparently means the *praetor urbanus*. See L155, B1.

ing taxes and aids on subjects or exempting them; granting pardons and dispensations against the rigor of the law; determining the name, value, and measure of the coinage; requiring subjects and liege vassals to swear that they will be loyal without exception [224] to the person to whom their oath is owed. These are the true prerogatives of sovereignty, which are included in the power to give law to all in general and to each in particular, and not to receive law from anyone but God.[12] For the prince or duke, who has power to give law to all his subjects in general and to each in particular, is not sovereign if he also takes law from a superior or an equal – I include equal because to have a companion is to have a master* – and he is even less a sovereign if he has this power only in the capacity of a vicar, lieutenant, or regent.

But since the word law is too general, it is best to specify the rights of sovereignty which are included, as I have said, in the lawmaking
6} power of the sovereign. Thus declaring war or making peace is one of the most important points of majesty, since it often entails the ruin or the preservation of a state. This is confirmed not only by the laws of the Romans, but also by those of every other people. Since there is more risk in beginning a war than in making peace, the commoners at Rome could make peace, but if it was a question of war, the great Estates {*comitia centuriata*} had to be assembled up until the time that the commoners obtained full lawmaking power. This is why the war against Mithridates was declared by the *lex Manilia*; against the pirates, by the *lex Gabinia*; against King Philip II of Macedon, by the *lex Sulpicia*. Peace was made with the Carthaginians by the *lex Marcia*, and there were others.[13] And because Caesar waged war in France
7} without a mandate from the people, Cato recommended that the army be called back and Caesar turned over to the enemy. In like manner, the assembly of the Athenian people declared war and made peace, as one can see in the war against the Megarians, against the Syracusans, and against the kings of Macedonia.

I take my examples from the two greatest democracies that ever were, because for a royal state there is no doubt. Indeed, sovereign princes take cognizance even of the minor actions and initiatives that are necessary in a war; whatever commission their deputies may have

*L155, C10–11 refines this to, "I have mentioned having an equal because someone who has an associate in the same jurisdiction, without whose support and consent he can command nothing and do nothing, has a kind of superior."

been given to make peace or conclude an alliance, they still do not agree to anything without notifying the prince. Thus at the recent treaty of Cambrai, we see the deputies for the king [225] writing back hourly to report all the proposals made on either side. But in a democracy, we most often see war and peace handled by decree of the senate, or privy council, acting alone, and very often by the decision of a single commander (*capitaine*) to whom full power is granted for that purpose. For there is nothing so dangerous in war as to make one's enterprises public, which cannot then succeed, any more than mines that have been exposed. Yet they would have to be divulged if the people is to be informed of them. This is why we read, in Greek and Latin histories, that the plans and strategies of war were always decided by commanders – and sometimes, if it was an important matter, by the advice of the senate – without ever consulting the people. But this was done, of course, only after the war was begun and publicly announced to the enemy by command of the people.

If someone tells me that the Roman Senate decided war and peace without notifying the people, I will not deny it. Yet it was an encroachment on the people's majesty; and the tribunes of the people used to intervene against it, as one sees in Titus Livy, who says, *Controversia*
{498} *fuit utrum populi iussu indiceretur, an satis esset S.C. Pervicere Tribuni, ut Quintus Consul de bello ad populum ferret: omnes centuriae iussere.** Furthermore, the Senate itself ordinarily preferred not to declare war without the people having ordered it. Thus Titus Livy, speaking of the Second Punic War, says, *Latum inde ad populum vellent iuberent populo Carthaginensi bellum indici*;† and in another place, *Ex S.C. populi iussu bellum Praenestinis indictum*;‡ and elsewhere, *Ex authoritate patrum populus Palaepolitanis bellum fieri iussit*;§ and again, *Populus bellum fieri Aequis iussit*;¶ and against the Samnites, *Patres solenni more*

* "There was a dispute as to whether war was [always] declared by order of the people, or whether a Senate decree was sufficient. The tribunes succeeded in having Quintus, the consul, put the question of war before the people, and it was ordered by all the centuries."

† "Then the people was asked whether it wished to order a declaration of war against the Carthaginian people."

‡ "By Senate decree war was declared against the Praenestines by order of the people." (Reference to Senatorial approval in this and other declarations stems from a time when an act of the people still required preliminary authorization by the Senate.)

§ "By authority of the fathers the people ordered war against the Palaepolitans."

¶ "The people ordered war against the Aequi."

indicto decreverunt, ut de ea re ad populum ferretur;* and against the Hernici, *Populus hoc bellum frequens iussit*;† and against the Vestini, *Bellum ex authoritate patrum populus adversus Vestinos iussit*.‡ Similarly, we read in the life of Pyrrhus that when the senate of Tarentum recommended that war be declared against the Romans, it was the people who gave the order. Titus Livy in Book 31 says that the Aetolians prohibited the making of any decision on peace or war, *nisi in Panaetolio, et Pylaico concilio*.§ This is why in the kingdoms of Poland, Denmark, and Sweden **[226]**, where the nobility makes claims to sovereignty, the kings can undertake a war only if it is decreed by the Estates, unless it is a case of urgent necessity, as provided in the ordinance of Casimir the Great [of Poland].

9} It is true that for making peace at Rome, the Senate very often acted without going to the people, as can be seen in the treaties concluded between the Romans and the Latins. In the Social War,[14] the Senate bypassed the people on almost all the treaties of peace and alliance; and captains often acted without the consent of the Senate, especially if the war was in a far distant country. In the Second Punic War, for example, the three Scipios concluded treaties of peace and alliance with the peoples and princes of Spain and Africa without the advice of the Senate. It is true that the Senate, and very often the people, authorized their actions and ratified the treaties after they were made, and if they were disadvantageous to the public paid no regard to them. But in this case the hostages [if any] and the captains had to answer to the enemy. Thus Mancinus, the consul, was handed over to the enemy on account of the peace he had agreed to with the Numantines, which the people refused to ratify. This is the point made by a Carthaginian senator to the Roman ambassadors, *Vos enim quod C. Luctatius primo nobiscum foedus icit, quia neque authoritate patrum, nec populi iussu ictum erat, negastis vos eo teneri. Itaque aliud foedus publico consilio ictum est*.¶ And the same author [Livy], speaking about Manlius, the governor of [the province of] Asia, says, *Gallograe-*

* "The fathers in a solemn declaration decreed that the matter should be taken to the people."

† "The people turned out in great numbers to order this war."

‡ "Acting by authority of the fathers, the people ordered war against the Vestines."

§ "except in the Panaetolican and Pylaican council."

¶ "You deny that you are bound by the treaty that the consul, C. Luctatius, entered into with us because it was done without the authority of the fathers or order of the people. Therefore, another treaty was concluded in public council."

*cis, inquit, bellum illatum, non ex Senatus authoritate, non populi iussu: quod quis unquam de sua sententia facere ausus est?** In a similar case, the consul Spurius Posthumius and his army, surprised by the enemy in the rocky passes of the Appenines, made peace with them. But when he returned to Rome with his troops disarmed, the Senate refused to ratify the peace agreement. The consul Posthumius then went before
{500} the people and said, *Cum me seu turpi, seu necessaria sponsione obstrinxi, qua tamen, quando inussu populi facta est, non tenetur populus Romanus, nec quicquam ex ea praeterquam corpora nostra debentur Samnitibus, dedamur per fetiales nudi vinctique.*† Thus the consul does not say it was a peace treaty, but only a simple promise, which he calls a *sponsio*. In fact, the enemy made the consuls and all **[227]** the captains and lieutenants of the army swear to it, and took six hundred hostages whom they might put to death if the people refused to ratify the agreement. But they made a serious mistake in not requiring all of the soldiers to take an oath obligating them either to return to the narrow passes and gorges of the mountains in the same condition as they then were, or else to return as prisoners if the people would not accept the agreement made by the captains. For the Senate and the people would undoubtedly have sent them back too, as they did with the consul and the six hundred hostages who had taken an oath. In a similar situation those [soldiers] who wanted to break the promise they had sworn to Hannibal were sent back bound hand and foot.

The people could also have ratified the agreement {with the Samnites}. That is what King Louis XII did concerning the treaty concluded at Dijon with the Swiss by the lord of Trimouille; by its terms, the chief officers of the army were given as hostages to the Swiss who, if the king did not ratify the agreement, had the right to put them to death. On the other hand, the duke of Anjou exercised that right against the hostages that were given to him by the forces
{501} besieged in the castle of Erval. When he saw that Robert Knolles, the

* "War, he said, was waged against the Galatians without authorization of the Senate and without a command of the people. Has anyone ever dared to do anything like that on his own?" L157, B10–11 adds, "This criticism of the absent Manlius by an adversary is a rhetorical exaggeration because this was sometimes done, as we have shown by our examples."

† "The promise to which I bound myself may have been shameful or it may have been necessary, but in any event it is not binding on the Roman people since it was not done by order of the people. And since we owe nothing by it to the Samnites except our bodies, let us be turned over to them naked and in chains by the *fetiales*."

castle's commander, who had arrived in the castle after the agreement was made, had chosen to prevent its surrender on the grounds that the defenders could not capitulate without his approval, the duke had the heads of the prisoners cut off.

If it were otherwise, and commanders were permitted to make peace treaties without a mandate or express ratification, they could obligate both peoples and sovereign princes at the enemy's pleasure and desire and on any conditions that they pleased. But that is absurd, since the acts of an agent may be disavowed if he has transacted even the slightest business for someone else without express authorization.

I will be told that these rules do not apply in Venice, where the senate has complete control of making peace or war, or in the leagues of the Swiss and Grisons, whose states are democratic. And when popular liberty was restored in Florence at the urging of Pier Soderini, it was decreed that the people would be involved only in making law, choosing magistrates, and laying taxes, contributions, and subsidies; the making of war and peace, or anything else concerning the [safety of] the state, would be left with the senate. My answer is that, for democratic and aristocratic states, the difficulty of assembling the people and the danger of exposing **[228]** secrets and initiatives leads the people to put the senate in charge of making war. Yet it is well understood that the commissions and mandates that are given
2} for this purpose derive from the people's authority and are dispatched in the name of the people by the senate, which is only the deputy and agent of the people and takes its authority from it, as do all the magistrates.*

As for monarchies, there is no difficulty at all in showing that the decision as to peace and war depends on the sovereign prince. But that is only if the monarchy is pure. In the kingdoms of Poland, Denmark, and Sweden, where the form of state is uncertain and changeable, according to whether the prince or the nobility is [momentarily the] stronger, but inclines more to aristocracy than monarchy, the determination of peace and war depends on the nobility, as we shall show in due course. We have already touched on the fact that the consent of the nobility is required to make law in

*L158, C3–5 makes it clear that the power of war and peace must remain in the people or nobility residually by adding, "but in either form of state [that is, aristocracy or democracy] the right and power of making war or concluding peace cannot be taken from the nobles or the people if their sovereignty is to be preserved."

these countries. This is why, in treaties of peace concluded with them, the seals of princes, counts, barons, palatines, castellans, and other dignitaries, are affixed. The recent treaty between the Poles and the Prussians, for example, carried the seals of one hundred and three noblemen of the country [Poland], a proceeding that is not found in other kingdoms.

The third prerogative of sovereignty is to establish the principal officers [of state], and is never questioned in so far as it applies to [appointment to] the highest magistracies.* The first law made by P. Valerius after driving the kings out of Rome was that the magistrates should be chosen by the people. The same law, Contarini tells us, was promulgated at Venice when they met to establish their commonwealth, and it is very strictly kept. It is still better kept in monarchies, where even very minor officers like doorkeepers, sergeants, clerks, trumpeters, and criers, who used to be appointed and dismissed by the magistrates at Rome, are appointed by the prince. Even inspectors of weights and measures, surveyors, cattle
{503} inspectors (*langayeurs*),[15] and other officials of that sort have been constituted as regular offices by continuing [royal] edicts.

I have said "principal officers," that is to say the highest magistrates, for there is no state in which the highest magistrates and many guilds and corporations are not permitted to create various minor officers, as I have shown above in reference to Rome. **[229]** But they do this in virtue of their office, and as though they were deputies who were created with the power of naming substitutes. We shall also see that feudal lords having the power to hold court (*seigneurs iusticiers*), even though they render fealty and homage to the sovereign jurisdiction of the prince, have power nonetheless to establish judges and officers. But this power is conceded to them by the sovereign prince. For it is quite certain that dukes, marquesses, counts, barons, and castellans were only judges and officers when they were originally instituted, as we shall show in due course.[16]†

Similarly, we read that the people of Carthage customarily chose five magistrates to elect the one hundred and four magistrates of the commonwealth, as is done in Nuremberg where the censors, who are elected by the Great Council, elect the new senators and then lay

*L158, D7 adds, "which are not held by authority of any other magistrates."
†L159, A8–9 adds, "But in a democracy the power of creating magistrates is sometimes vested in the higher magistrates."

down their authority. The senate of twenty-six members then chooses the eight Ancients, the Thirteen, and also the seven burgomasters, as well as the twelve judges for civil and the five for criminal cases. This was also a regular power of the Roman censors, who filled out the numerical strength of the Senate at their discretion, as the consuls earlier used to do by sufferance of the people who, in the beginning, as Festus Pompeius tells us, used to do this by itself. Sometimes a dictator was named only to fill out the senate, as when Fabius Buteo, named dictator by the consul Terentius in accordance with a decree of the Senate, chose one hundred and seventy-seven senators in one stroke. It is true that a senator, strictly speaking, was
4} not a magistrate, as we will show in our chapter on the senate. But however this may be, those [magistrates] who appointed senators had that power only from the people, and it was revocable at the people's pleasure.

The same may be said of the cadilesqueri in Turkey, who are like two chancellors of the king and can appoint and remove all the cadis and paracadis, or judges. In Egypt, before Selim I conquered it, the grand edegnar, who was like the sultan's constable, had the power of supplying all the other officers, as in ancient times the mayors of the palace did in France. And not long ago, the chancellor of France had the power to fill, by preemption (*par prévention*),* all offices **[230]** that carried no stipend and also offices for which the stipend did not exceed twenty-five *livres*, a privilege that was revoked by King Francis I. The chancellor, to be sure, as well as the great edegnar and the great mayor of the palace, were always appointed by the king. Yet the very great power that they had was extremely harmful to our early kings and to the sultans. Since that time, the mode of appointments has been reformed, so that even the lieutenants of the *bailliages* and *seneschaussées*,[17] who used to be appointed by the *baillis* and *seneschaux* before the time of Charles VII, are now appointed by the king and have the status of officers.

It can also happen that magistrates, or guilds and corporations, may have the power to choose and name high magistrates. Thus we read in the registers of the court that by an ordinance of 1408, it was decided that the officers of the Parlement would be elective, and the chancellor

*L159, C7–10 omits *prévention* as the basis of this power of the chancellor. *Prévention* was the right of a higher authority (typically a court) to remove an affair from the purview of a lower authority otherwise entitled to handle it.

was ordered to go to the Parlement for elections to vacant offices.
{505} The same ordinance was repeated by King Louis XI in 1465. After him, in the time of Charles VIII, not only were the presidents, counsellors, and advocates of the king elected, but in 1496, election was also extended to the king's attorney-general (who alone among members of the judicial establishment of the Parlement of Paris [*corps de la cour*] takes an oath to the king only, whereas the [king's] attorneys of the other Parlements, who are called substitutes, take their oaths to the court). But the conveyances (*provisions*) and letters of office confirming the elections, were, and still are, always granted by the king.

This last will serve as a reply to anyone who objects that Duke Arthur of Brittany was elected constable of France by the votes of all the princes, the Great Council, and the Parlement in 1424. Although the king was mentally deranged at that time, and the seals of France stamped with the image of the queen, the king's sword was delivered in trust to Arthur, who was to hold it of the king in fealty and liege homage and to be the chief commander in war over all others except the king.* One might still object that the great palatine of Hungary, who is the highest magistrate in Hungary and the king's lieutenant-general, is elected by the Estates of the land. That is true enough. Yet the conveyance, installation, and confirmation of the office belongs to the king, who is the principal and chief author of his power. **[231]** The Estates of the kingdom of Hungary, however, still contend that they have the right of electing their kings, which the house of Austria denies, and it seems as though the kings [of Hungary] have tolerated the election of the great palatine to make them forget about electing the king. But they are so stubborn that they have preferred to give themselves up to the Turks {in a kind of protectorate} rather than lose that right.

It is therefore not the election of officers that implies the right of sovereignty, but rather the confirmation and conferment of the office. Yet the power to elect has something sovereign about it, and shows
{506} that princes are not absolutely sovereign unless such elections take place only by their will and consent. Thus by an ordinance of Sigismund Augustus, all officers in the kingdom of Poland are to be

* "... the king's sword ... the king." L160, A5–7 gives a more cautious and less clearcut version of the grant: "Nevertheless the new constable, in taking custody of the royal sword and leadership of the royal army, took an oath to uphold the laws and in that very moment acknowledged that he had his magistracy and authority from the king."

elected by the Estates of each province, and yet they are to have their letters of conferment from the king.* Nor is this something new. Going back to the time of the Goths, we read in Cassiodorus that Theodoric, king of the Goths, gave letters of confirmation to officers whom the Senate had elected, and in [one of his] letters addressed to the Senate, used these words with respect to someone on whom he had conferred the dignity of patrician: *Iudicium vestrum P.C. noster comitatur assensus.*† Since the power of commanding all the subjects of a state belongs to him who holds the sovereignty, it is important that all magistrates should acknowledge that their power is from him.‡

Now let us speak of yet another sovereign prerogative, namely, the right of judging in last instance [or final appeal] (*dernier ressort*, *extrema provocatio*), which has always been one of the principal rights of sovereignty. Thus, after the Romans drove out their kings, not only was judgment without appeal reserved to the Roman people by the *lex Valeria*, but also [the right to hear an] appeal from any magistrate. Because the consuls often contravened that law, it was thrice repromulgated, and by the *lex Duilia*, the penalty of death was
:07} established for transgressing it. Titus Livy called this law the foundation of popular liberty, even though it was poorly enforced. In Athens, the same law was observed more strictly, and, as Xenophon and Demosthenes indicate, the right of judging in the last instance was reserved to the people by appeal not only from all the magistrates, but from all the cities of their allies. **[232]** Moreover, we find much the same arrangement recorded in Contarini, namely that the first law made [by the Venetians] in setting up their state, was that appeal should lie from every magistrate to the Great Council. We also read that Francesco Valori, duke of Florence, was killed for no other

*For "yet the power to elect . . . from the king" L160, B7–C3 substitutes, "But if this right of election (*ea creatio*) had been assigned to the people or corporations by those who founded the state and the laws in such fashion that it could not be taken away from the corporations or the people, then the prince would not really have the rights of sovereignty, because the magistrate would have to take his authority from the people, not the prince. That is what happened gradually to the kings of Poland. For when, by a law of Sigismund Augustus, all the magistrates were appointed in the council and by the vote of each province, the sovereignty of the kings, who also reigned by favor of the people [that is, were elected], was very much impaired."

†"Our consent follows your judgment, Conscript Fathers."

‡For "Since . . . in him" L160, C8–9 substitutes, "Therefore, all the powers to command (*imperia*) of all the magistrates has to be conferred by him who holds the supreme power of the state."

reason than his failure to comply with an appeal taken from him to the Great Council of the people by three Florentines whom he had condemned to death.

Someone may object that not only the duke at Florence but also the dictator at Rome and other magistrates often ignored appeals, as can be seen in a number of historical accounts. Indeed, the Roman Senate, after it had surrounded and captured the legion that had been garrisoned at Reggio and brought it back to Rome, had all the soldiers and captains who survived whipped and beheaded {within the city limits} without heeding their appeals to the people or the opposition of the tribunes, who loudly protested that the sacred laws on appeal were being trampled under foot. Here, to be brief, I answer with Papinian that one must be guided not by what is done at Rome, but by
{*508*} what should be done, for it is quite certain that appeal from the Senate to the people did exist, and that the intercession of a tribune ordinarily brought the entire Senate to a halt, as we have indicated above. The first to give the Roman Senate the power to judge without appeal was the emperor Hadrian, since the ordinance of Caligula, which empowered all the magistrates to judge without appeal, was never put in execution. And although Nero decreed that the fines paid by those who appealed [without merit] to the Senate should be the same as if they had appealed to him personally, he did not remove the possibility of appeal from the Senate to him.

It may seem that this is directly contrary to what we have been saying.[18] For if there was no appeal from the Senate to the emperor, and if the right of judging in the last instance (*dernier ressort*) was thus in the Senate, then final appeal (*dernier appel*) is not a prerogative of sovereignty. In addition, the master of the palace, whom they called the *praefectus praetorio*, not only used to judge without appeal, but also heard appeals from all the magistrates and governors of the Empire, as Flavius Vopiscus reports. Indeed, in every state one finds [high] courts and Parlements that judge without appeal, such as the eight Parlements [233] of France, the four {high} Courts (*Cours*) in Spain, the Imperial Chamber in Germany, the Council at Naples, the Rota at Rome, and the senate at Milan. And in all the Imperial [that is, free] cities, duchies, and counties holding [immediately] of the Empire, there is no appeal to the Imperial Chamber in criminal cases that have been decided by the magistrates of the [territorial] princes and the

09} imperial cities. And it would not help to say that appeals lodged against *baillis*, *seneschaux*, and other lower judges do not go directly to the Parlements or to the Imperial Chamber,[19] but to the king or the emperor, who transmit the cases to judges whom they have deputed for this purpose, and who for this purpose are their lieutenants, so that in this case there cannot be an appeal from the lieutenant to the prince any more than from the prince himself. It is true that there is no appeal in terms of [civil] law from a lieutenant to the person who has deputized him. But all the appeal forms state that the condemned persons are appealing to the king and to the Parlements, which call themselves ordinary judges for ordinary cases, and not extraordinary judges only, especially since they judge many cases in the first instance.* Beyond that, one sees the magistrates of the lower presidial courts[20] judging in the last instance in certain cases. Hence it seems that judgment in the last instance is not a prerogative of sovereignty.

My reply to this is that the right of judgment in the last instance includes, along with appeal, the procedure of civil petition (*requeste civile, civilis suplicatio*)† which has led many jurists to conclude that civil petition is one of the rights of sovereignty. Although in proceedings by civil petition, judges {almost always} review their own decisions, the petition is nonetheless addressed to the sovereign prince who accepts or rejects it as he sees fit, and often has the case called up before him to confirm or quash the verdict that was given, or to deliver the case to other judges – which is the true mark of sovereignty and of judgment in the last instance.[21] Indeed, magistrates
10} do not have the power to change or correct their judgments without the permission of the sovereign prince, if they are not to incur the penalty of giving false judgment, as provided both by common law and by the ordinances of this kingdom. And although many judges have

*"And it would not help to say . . . in the first instance" is omitted at L161, C5. (The apparent point of the passage in the French is to construct [and then refute] a highly strained explanation of why the Parlements and similar high courts, despite all the appearances to the contrary, do not really have the right of judgment in the last instance. They are supposed to be acting not in their own right of office, but as special deputies. Bodin here seems not to be presenting any known interpretation of French procedure, but merely a construction of his own, which is put forward only to show that it is not a way out of the apparent difficulty.)

†L161, C7–8 adds, "by which one may petition the prince even when an appeal against the verdict of the higher magistrates (*contra sententiam maiorum magistratuum*) is not allowed."

adopted the custom of using the words "in sovereignty" in rendering their judgments, that is really to abuse **[234]** the term, which applies only to a sovereign prince.

Even if a sovereign prince should pass an edict ordering that there should be no procedure of appeal or of civil request from the magistrates to his person, as the Emperor Caligula sought to do, his subjects would still be allowed to present petitions to his majesty. For he cannot tie his hands, nor bar his subjects from proceedings of restitution, petition, or request, especially since all edicts dealing with appeals and judgments are no more than civil laws by which, as we have said, the prince cannot be bound. This is why the Privy Council, and the chancellor {Michel} de l'Hôpital especially, found it new and very strange that the commissioners appointed to try President[22] L'Alemant forbade him, in the verdict they handed down against him, to come any closer to the court than twenty leagues in order thereby to stop him from presenting a civil petition; this is something that even the king cannot take from his subject, although it is in his power to accept or reject the petition.

We also see that in all the appanages[23] given to children of the house of France and, generally, in the constitution of duchies, marquisates, counties, and principalities, it has always been the
{*511*} custom to reserve fealty and homage, judgment in the last instance, and sovereignty. Sometimes the reservation is only of judgment in the last instance and sovereignty, as in the declaration delivered by King Charles V to the duke of Berry on 3 March 1374. But fealty and homage were implied, since it is quite certain that the duchy of Berry was an appanage entrusted to the duke of Berry on condition of respecting royal rights and of reversion to the crown upon failure of heirs male, as I have learned from the letters of appanage, which are still extant in the treasury of France.*

There is also a similar declaration rendered by Archduke Philip of Austria to King Louis XII in 1499, and another declaration of 1505 by the same individual in which he recognizes the jurisdiction of the Parlement of Paris and promises to obey its decrees with respect to the counties of Artois and Flanders and other lands that he held of the king. And in the treaty of Arras made between King Charles VII and

*L162, B3–6 adds, "For although the term 'sovereignty' includes everything that we can show, by inference, to be supreme and primary in a state, the safeguard of appeal in last instance was customarily reserved in a special notation."

Philip II, duke of Burgundy, there is express reservation of fealty and homage, appeal, **[235]** and sovereignty for the lands which Philip acknowledged as held of the crown, by him as by his predecessors. And the main reason why King Charles V of France declared war on the king of England was that the latter ignored protests based on the treaty of Brétigny, which Charles V had not ratified without reserving the right of hearing appeals,* as can be seen by the decree of the Parlement given on 14 May 1370, in which the duchy of Aquitaine was forfeited to the king on this account.

If, on the contrary, a sovereign prince yields the right of last appeal and the sovereignty belonging to him, and gives it[24] to a vassal, he turns his subject into a sovereign prince, as King Francis I did in resigning all rights of fealty and homage, appeal, and sovereignty over Châtelet-sur-Moselle to the duke of Lorraine in 1517. But when he permitted this same duke to judge, condemn, and acquit in sovereign
512} capacity in the duchy of Bar, and when the duke's officers took this to be a consequence of his absolute sovereignty, the attorney general complained to the king. Whereupon Duke Anthony of Lorraine and, after him, Duke Francis, delivered an acknowledgment in due form by which they declared that they in no way intended to detract from the fealty and homage, right of appeal, and sovereignty that they owed the crown in consideration of the said duchy, and that they had exercised judgment in sovereign degree by sufferance only. These letters of acknowledgment were subsequently presented to the privy council in 1564.†

The best expedient for preserving the state is never to grant a prerogative of sovereignty to any subject, much less a stranger, for it is a stepping stone to sovereignty. On this account [the Parlement] raised many difficulties about approving the letters for the Exchequer of Alençon because of the way they prejudiced the right of last

*For "was that ... appeals" L162, C7–9 substitutes, more specifically, "because the English magistrates and governors who governed Aquitania under fealty to the French would not permit appeals by their subjects (*provocantes subditos non exaudirent*)."

†L162, D13–L163, A6 adds, "[This was during the reign of] King Charles IX, who tried everything to give Duke Charles of Lorraine an extremely generous charter conveying the duchy of Bar in right of sovereignty. But it was in vain because there is no way that a king can separate the rights of sovereignty from his person, not even, indeed, if the Parlement of Paris consents (even though the authority or power of that court is as nothing when the prince is there, for in his presence all the powers of all the magistrates are suspended)."

appeal.* This seemed so serious that one of the king's advocates said in full council that it would be better to introduce a dozen [new] Parlements,[25] even though appeal in certain cases and for many kinds of causes was reserved along with fealty and homage.[26] In fact the kings of England and the dukes of Burgundy found yet another reason to form an alliance and make war against the king of France in his refusal to give them the privilege of the exchequer that he had
{513} given **[236]** to the dukes of Alençon, so that no appeal could be taken from their judges and magistrates. For the officers of the dukes and counts, and even the dukes themselves, were summoned to appear before the king to witness the correction and amendment of their judgments, which is a mark of subjection that sorely grieved them; sometimes they were made to appear before the king for affairs of little consequence. When the dukes of Brittany complained of this to Philip the Fair and Philip the Tall, the kings sent letters patent to the court of Parlement, in February 1306 and October 1316 respectively, by which they declared that they did not wish the duke of Brittany or his officers to be summoned before them except for cases of denial of justice and false judgment, or for cases involving sovereignty. By these same letters one can see how the confirmation of last resort and sovereignty was implied by the exception of reserved cases.

We may reach the same conclusion with respect to all the princes and lords [of Germany] from whom appeal lies to the Empire and the Imperial Chamber. They are not sovereign, since it would be an act of treason, punishable by death, to lodge an appeal against a sovereign prince, unless it was the kind of appeal adopted by that Greek who appealed from King Philip of Macedon counselled ill to that same king counselled well. It was in this form that the attorneys for Louis de Bourbon {prince of Condé} worded his appeal from an interlocutory decree rendered by King Francis II in his privy council. It is a form that the jurist Baldus finds proper and acceptable, and it is fully consistent with the majesty of a sovereign prince to follow the example
{514} of the king {of Macedonia} and to accept the appeal. But if princes, wishing not to seem changeable and vacillating, want their decrees to stand, they should act the way that same king did toward Machetas.

* "On this account . . . appeal." L163, A8–B1 expands and clarifies, "On this account it was long debated in the Parlement (*senatu*) whether Francis d'Alençon (who made me his master of requests and a member of his council) should be granted jurisdiction without appeal in his province, as had been traditionally permitted to the ancient dukes."

Having condemned him unjustly, he compensated Machetas from his own resources without repealing or changing his verdict.

A consequence of this prerogative of sovereignty is the power of granting pardons to the condemned, ignoring verdicts and going against the rigor of the laws to save them from death, loss of goods, dishonor, or exile. [This is the fifth mark of sovereignty] for it is not in the power of any of the magistrate, no matter how great, to do any such thing, or to alter anything in the judgments he has handed down. Although the proconsuls and provincial governors had **[237]** as much judicial power (*iurisdiction*) as all the magistrates of Rome put together, they were not even permitted to reinstate exiles banished for a limited time, as we read in the letters of Pliny the Younger, the governor of [the province of] Asia, to the emperor Trajan; and much less were they allowed to pardon those condemned to death, which is a prohibition that applies to every magistrate in every state.

It may appear that the dictator Papirius Cursor granted a pardon to Fabius Maximus, his master of the infantry,* who had given battle
515} against his orders but had killed twenty thousand of the enemy. But in effect it was the people that granted the pardon, even though it proceeded by earnestly entreating the dictator to forgive the error. Fabius had appealed to the people from the sentence of the dictator, and he in turn defended his verdict against the appellant, which shows that the power of life and death was in the people. We see also that Servius Galba, the orator, who had been accused of treason by Cato the Censor and convicted, had recourse to the mercy of the people, who granted him a pardon, which led Cato to say that if Galba had not had recourse to tears and to his children, he would have had a whipping.

Similarly, the Athenian people, alone and to the exclusion of the magistrates, had the power of granting pardons, as was shown in the case of Demosthenes, Alcibiades, and several others. In the commonwealth of Venice too, it is only the Great Council of all the gentlemen of Venice that grants pardons. At one time the Council of Ten used to grant them by sufferance [of the Council],† but it was decided in 1523 that the giunta of thirty-two members should attend the Council {of Ten}, and that no pardon should be valid unless

*L164, A8 corrects this to "master of the horse" (which was the title of the official appointed by the dictator as his military aide).

†For "by sufferance [of the Council]" L164, C4 substitutes, "by abusing its power."

everyone consented, and in 1562 the Council {of Ten} was forbidden to take any initiative whatever. And although the emperor Charles V, in constituting the senate of Milan, granted it all the prerogatives of sovereignty as his vicar and lieutenant, he reserved the right of pardon for himself, as I have learned from the letters patent that he issued. This is something that is strictly observed in all monarchies. And although in Florence, under the democracy, the Eight had usurped
{*516*} the power of granting pardons, it was restored to the people when Soderini reformed the state.

As for our kings, there is nothing of which they are more **[238]**
jealous, and they have never suffered seigneurial judges to review letters of remission granted by the king, although they could review letters of pardon.[27] King Francis I gave his mother the power to grant pardons, but the court [Parlement] drew up a remonstration to the king protesting that this was one of the fairest marks of sovereignty and could not be shared with a subject without diminishing his majesty; the queen mother, being advised of it, renounced the privilege and returned the letters to the king before the protest could be presented to him. For not even the queen of France can have that privilege, or indeed any of the other prerogatives of sovereignty. The law of the Romans, by which the empress was dispensed from edicts and ordinances, does not hold in this kingdom, and there is a decree in the registers of the court for July 1465 in which the queen was required to furnish a deposit for the debt stipulated in a contract, no regard being paid to her claim of privilege.

{*517*} I am well aware that King Charles VI, without a single member of the Great Council being present, issued letters patent on 13 March 1401, giving Arnaud de Corbie, the chancellor of France, the power of granting pardons and remissions. But this was at a time when the chancellors were all-powerful, and King Charles VI was under tutelage because of his {mental} illness. Someone may still object that provincial governors gave pardons in olden times, as one can still see in the Customs of Hainaut and in the ancient Customs of Dauphiné. And the bishop of Embrun cites authentic charters in pretending to this right.

I answer that such customs and privileges are abuses and encroachments, which were legitimately suppressed by an edict of Louis XII in 1499. And if privileges of that sort are void, we may say that the confirmations are also void, for the confirmation is never valid if the

privilege is worthless in itself. And void it surely is since the right of pardon cannot be given away without giving up the crown itself. It is different, however, with governors, vicars, and lieutenant-generals of sovereign princes, since they have that power neither by privilege nor by right of office,* but by commission, as do the princes, vicars, **[239]** and lieutenants of the [German] Empire. Yet in a well-ordered state, this power ought not to be conceded to anyone either by commission
8} or by right of office, except to establish a regent where that is required because the prince is too far away or because he is a captive, a madman, or a minor. This is what was done for Louis IX, whom the Estates of France placed under the tutelage of his mother, Blanche of Castile, after having charged several princes with seeing that she did not grant her guardianship to any other persons. Similarly, Charles of France was regent in France during the captivity of King John; Louise of Savoy was regent during the imprisonment of King Francis I, with full royal rights in her capacity as regent; and the duke of Bedford was regent in France during the illness of the king {Charles VI}.

Here someone may object that notwithstanding the ordinance of Louis XII, the cathedral chapter of the church of Rouen still claims the privilege of granting pardons in honor of St. Roman. On the eve of that saint's holiday they forbid all judges, including even the Parlement of Rouen, to carry out sentences of death, as I saw at first hand when I was there as a commissioner charged with the general reformation of Normandy.† And when the court, after the holiday had passed,‡ ignored the pardon issued by the chapter and ordered the execution of someone it had condemned, the chapter complained to the king. One of the princes of the blood headed the chapter's delega-

*". . . since they have that power neither by privilege nor by right of office." L165, B9–12 holds the contrary, "But deputies of the prince or administrators (*procuratores*) of the kingdom claim prerogatives of sovereignty not by the favor of the prince, but by right of magistracy or public charge (*sed iure magistratus aut publicae curationis*), as do those who call themselves the vicars of the [German] Empire." (The restriction on possession of this power has thus been weakened. The change is perhaps prompted by Bodin's reflection that the powers of the great German princes could not be reduced to mere commissions and were held by right of office.)

†For "as a commissioner . . . Normandy" L165, D5 substitutes, more modestly, "as a commissioner for enforcing royal fiscal rights." (This was a royal mission entrusted to Bodin in 1570.)

‡"after the holiday had passed" is eliminated in the Latin. L165, D6–7 reads, "And when the court executed some condemned persons in defiance of the prohibition."

tion, while the Parlement sent a deputation that included the king's advocate, Bigot, who heavily emphasized the abuse of, and encroachment upon, the king's majesty. But the times were unfavorable, and despite these earnest remonstrations, the privilege has remained.* It is a privilege that is perhaps modelled on that accorded the vestals at Rome, who could pardon someone about to be executed, if one of the vestals happened to cross his path by chance, as Plutarch reports in
{519} his life of Numa. This is a custom still observed at Rome, when they come upon a cardinal in taking someone to be executed.

The worst thing about the privilege of St. Roman is that they pardon only the most abominable crimes that they can find, crimes that **[240]** the king customarily did not pardon. [And this leads me to observe that] many sovereign princes abuse their power in this area, believing that a pardon is the more pleasing to God as the trespass is the more detestable. But I maintain – until such time as I hear a better argument – that a sovereign prince cannot remit a penalty established by the law of God any more than he can dispense from the law of God, to which he is subject. If a magistrate deserves capital punishment for dispensing from the ordinance of his king, how can a sovereign prince be permitted to dispense a subject from the law of God? And if a prince cannot sacrifice the civil interest of a subject [by a pardon], how could he forgive the penalty that God ordains by His law? Thus premeditated murder deserves death by the law of God, but oh, how many pardons do we see!

But how, someone will say, can the prince show his mercy if he cannot remit penalties established by the law of God? I reply that there are many ways, and that they arise from violations of the civil
{520} laws. For example, if the prince has forbidden his subjects to bear arms or to deliver foodstuffs to the enemy on pain of death, he would make good use of his power in pardoning someone who took up arms only in self-defense, or who was driven by poverty and dire need to sell dear to the enemy. Or if the penalty for theft is death according to the civil law, a benevolent prince can reduce it to payment of fourfold restitution, which is the penalty stated in the law of God and also in the common law [of peoples].

But as for the murderer by premeditation, "You shall drag him from my holy altar, 'says the law [of God],' and you shall have no pity

*L165, D11–12 adds, "But here I should advise the reader that, while I was translating this into Latin, this privilege was removed by King Henry III."

on him but shall put him to death, and then will I shed my great mercy upon you." Nevertheless, on Good Friday, Christian princes grant pardons only for things that are unpardonable. Yet pardons for such misdeeds bring with them plagues, famines, wars, and the ruin of states. That is why the law of God says that by punishing those who have deserved death, one removes the curse that lies upon the people. For of a hundred wicked deeds, not even two are brought to justice; of those that get there, half cannot be proven; and if proven crimes are pardoned, what punishment will there be to serve as an example **[241]** to the wicked?

Indeed, when offenders are unable to obtain pardon from their own prince, they interpose the favor of another. The Estates of Spain thus complained to the Catholic king {Philip} and requested him to instruct his ambassador to the king of France {Henry II} not to accept or to forward any more requests asking pardon from the king of Spain for condemned persons who had fled to France. For having obtained their pardons, they often killed the judges who had convicted them.* But of all the pardons that a prince can grant, none is more seemly than one given for an injury done to his person, and of all
1} capital punishments there is none more agreeable to God than one established for injury done to His majesty. But what can one hope for from a prince who cruelly avenges his own injuries and pardons others, including even those done directly against the honor of God?

What we have said about the power of pardon and remission belonging only to the prince may work to the detriment of lords who have the power of confiscating the goods of criminals, since they are never permitted to question or obstruct a pardon, as is clear from a decree of the Parlement. Under the notion of pardon, furthermore, many would include the restitution of minors and adults, [and] the benefit of age, which in many states are reserved for the sovereign
2} prince.† But except for the restitution of bastards, fiefs,‡ and things like that, these are not marks of sovereignty. The magistrates had that

*For "The Estates of Spain . . . convicted them" L166, D7–10 substitutes and clarifies, "Hence the complaints of the Spaniards against King Henry II of France, who persuaded King Philip II to pardon a number of exiles who then returned home and killed the judges [who had condemned them]."

†"Under the notion . . . many states." L167, A6–8 reads, "Many would extend the term remission (*restitutio*) to civil judgments, as when someone has been deceived and cheated for want of counsel, or when someone asks for indulgence in consideration of his youth."

‡"fiefs" is omitted at L167, B1.

sort of power at Rome. By an ordinance of Charles VII and Charles VIII, judges are expressly instructed to pay no attention to what are called letters of justice (*lettres de justice*) unless they are equitable.[28] This is already implied by the words "So far as may suffice" (*Tant qu'a suffire doive*), which appear in all letters of justice granted in this kingdom. But if that clause is not affixed, the magistrate has cognizance only of the issue of fact, the penalty being reserved to the law and the right of pardon to the sovereign. That is why Cicero, asking Caesar to pardon Ligarius, says "I have often pleaded before judges as your adversary, and never did I say on behalf of my client, 'Pardon him, gentlemen. He has erred; he didn't mean it; he will never again etc.,' as though it is a father of whom pardon is asked. Before judges one says that the charge **[242]** was fabricated out of envy, that the accuser is a slanderer, that the witnesses are false," whereby Cicero shows that Caesar, being sovereign, had power to grant a pardon,* which judges do not.

As for fealty and liege homage, it too, as we have shown above,[29] is clearly one of the greatest rights of sovereignty when it is rendered to someone without exception.

As for the right of coining money, it is of the same nature as law, and only he who has the power to make law can regulate the coinage. That is readily evident from the Greek, Latin, and French terms, for the word *nummus* [in Latin] is from the Greek word *nomos*, and [the
{523} French] *loi* (law) is at the root of *aloi* (alloy), the first letter of which is dropped by those who speak precisely.† Indeed, after law itself, there is nothing of greater consequence than the title, value, and measure of coins, as we have shown in a separate treatise,[30] and in every well-ordered state, it is the sovereign prince alone who has this power. This, we read, is the way it was at Rome. When a value was set for the {silver} victory {*victoriatus*}, it was done by an express law of the people. Although the Senate, to provide for public necessities, issued its own decree making a half-pound of copper worth as much as a pound – and later on a quarter, until at last an ounce was given the value of a pound – this was all done with the consent of the tribunes, as we have said above. Later on, the emperor Constantine ordered

*For "had power to grant a pardon" L167, C2 substitutes as the equivalent, "had the power of life and death (*vitae ius ac necis habuisse*)."

†The prime meaning of the term *aloi* in French is the statutory degree of purity in gold and silver. The digression on these French terms is dropped at L167, C9, perhaps because they are not the roots of any French word for money.

that counterfeiters should be punished as though guilty of treason, which is a practice that princes carefully maintain, reserving the punishment of counterfeiters for themselves to the exclusion of all other lords. And the same punishment is meted out [even] to those who have coined good money without the prince's leave.

It is true that in this kingdom many private persons once had the power* to coin money, among others the viscount of Touraine; the bishops of Meaux, Cahors, Agde, and Embrun; and the counts of Saint Paul, la Marche, Nevers, and Blois. But a general edict of King Francis I suppressed all these privileges, which could not properly
4} have been granted and which, if granted, the law declares invalid. Furthermore, privileges run only for the lifetime of those who grant them, as we showed in discussing the nature of privileges. In any event, this right and prerogative of sovereignty **[243]** ought never to be shared with a subject, as was made quite clear to King Sigismund Augustus of Poland, who had given the duke of Prussia the privilege of coining money in 1543. The Estates of the country issued a decree in which a statement was inserted that the king could not bestow this right on anyone since it was inseparable from the crown. For the same reason, the archbishop of Gnezna in Poland and the archbishop of Canterbury in England, both chancellors, having obtained this same prerogative, were subsequently deprived of it. For that cause also the cities of Italy, which held of the Empire and had usurped this right, were required by the Treaty of Constance to surrender it to the emperor (who nonetheless granted the privilege to the people of Lucca as a favor to Pope Lucius III, a native of that city). We read also that the main pretext seized upon by King Peter of Aragon for driving King James of Majorca out of his kingdom was that James had coined money, which Peter claimed he had no right to do. And one of the occasions taken by Louis XI to make war on Francis, duke of Brittany, was that the latter had minted coins of gold in contravention of a treaty made in 1465. Throughout the Roman Empire, it may be
5} noted, the right of minting coins of gold was reserved.† And although John, duke of Berry, had the privilege of coinage in either metal from King Charles V of France, his fear of forfeiture led him to strike gold

*"... had the power." L167, D10 clarifies this by speaking of those who "held this benefice by abuse (*eo beneficio abutebantur*)."

†L168, B7–9 explains this by substituting, "The Romans, when they permitted copper and silver coins to be struck in all their provinces, forbade making them of gold."

coins bearing the figure of a sheep (*moutons d'or*) that were of the finest gold ever seen before or since in this kingdom.

For whatever privilege be granted to the subject with respect to coining money, the law and value of it always depends on the sovereign. Hence the only thing within the subject's power is the stamp, which in ancient Rome was at the discretion of the masters of the mint (*maistres de monnoye*, *triumviri monetales*), who put whatever stamp they wished upon the coins and their names as well, together with the letters "IIIviri A.A.A.F.F." The *bailli* of the mountains {*bailli* of Dauphiné} interprets this as *aere argento auro flavo ferunto*,* instead of *auro argento aere flando feriundo*,† which is what he ought to have said. For sovereign princes used not to care about having their likeness engraved on their coins; King Servius, who was the first to put a stamp on money, which was merely of simple copper, had the figure of a bull engraved on it, in imitation of the Athenians who used that figure as well as an owl.

The kings and princes of the East, however, had their image put upon their coins, as did Philip **[244]**, king of Macedonia, on the gold coins called the *philippus*; and the kings of Persia on a coin bearing their image called the *dareikos*, of which they were so jealous that King Darius, Herodotus tells us, had Ariander, the governor of Egypt, beheaded for having coined money with his image on it. The emperor Commodus did the same to his favorite, Perennius, for a similar
{*526*} indiscretion. And although King Louis XII let the Genevans keep all their sovereign power, he forbade them to put anything other than his image on their money. In the past they had stamped it with a gibbet as a symbol of justice, and they do the same today since they do not want their money to bear the image of the duke [of Savoy].

If coinage is one of the rights of sovereignty, so too is the regulation of weights and measures, even though there is no lord so petty that he cannot pretend to this prerogative by the authority of local custom, to

* "working in copper, silver, and yellow gold." The text should read *ferundo* instead of *ferunto*, even though the latter is given in some half dozen editions of the *République* that I have checked. Professor Mark Petrini of the Columbia University Classics Department has informed me that *ferunto* could be a third person plural imperative. But since an imperative makes little sense here, I have preferred to assume a typographical error repeatedly passed over.

† "casting and striking in gold, silver, and copper." Mr. William Metcalf of the American Numismatic Society has informed me that Bodin's rendition is substantially correct except that the order of the metals, in a modern reading, would be "copper, silver, and gold."

the great detriment of the commonwealth. This is why King Philip the Fair, Philip the Tall, and Louis XI resolved that there would be only one system of weights and measures, and to this end all the feudal measures were equalized throughout most of the kingdom, as I have learned from the report of the commissioners taken from the *Chambre des Comptes*. But implementation proved more difficult than anticipated on account of the disputes and lawsuits that resulted from it. We read in Polybius, however, that this [uniformity] was effectively achieved for Achaia and Morea, where all the cities had the same money, weights, measures, customs, laws, religion, officers, and government.

As to the right of laying direct and indirect taxes (*tailles et imposts*)[31] on subjects, or exempting some of them, that too depends on the power of giving law and granting privileges. This is not to say that a commonwealth cannot exist without direct taxes (*tailles*), for President Lemaître writes that they have been levied in this kingdom only since St. Louis was king. But if there is need to impose them, or repeal them, it can be done only by whoever has the sovereign power, as was determined by a decree of the Parlement against the duke of Burgundy, and many times since, both in the Parlement and the privy council. As for the unauthorized taxes introduced by various private lords and the corporations and guilds of towns and villages, King Charles IX issued a general edict at the request of the Estates of Orléans [245] by which this was expressly forbidden unless special permission was given, although taxation for public needs without authorization by corporations and guilds was tolerated up to twenty-five pounds. The same edict was then reiterated at Moulins and is in accord with common law and the opinion of the jurists.

Although the Roman Senate in time of war, and even the censors, sometimes imposed taxes, knowing that the commoners if assembled would be reluctant to grant them, it was by sufferance of the tribunes of the people. The tribunes indeed often intervened to forestall that practice. They thus brought a proposal to the people that henceforth no one should presume to have a law passed in a military encampment; the Senate, in a clever move, had used that locale to publish a tax known as the twentieth on emancipations, with the excuse that it was for the purpose of paying the army (which readily approved it). But Roman history also shows us many occasions when charges and impositions were levied by the people itself. It was thus taxed (*taillé*) during the {second} Punic war; but after the return of the general, Paulus Emilius, who filled the city with booty taken from King Perseus of Macedonia, the people was freed of taxes up until the civil wars of the Triumvirate. In like manner, the emperor Pertinax, says Herodian, removed the charges, duties, and tolls that tyrants had placed upon the rivers, and on the entries and exits of towns, above and beyond the traditional levies.

Someone may object that many lords have obtained the right of levying taxes, duties, and tolls by prescription. And even in this kingdom it is evident that many lords can levy a direct tax (*taille*) in four circumstances confirmed by court decrees and customs, and that this holds even for lords that do not have the power to administer justice (*iurisdiction*).[32] I answer that this practice, which began as an abuse and has persisted for many years, has some color of prescription. But no abuse can become so inveterate that the law, by which abuses must
{*529*} be regulated, does not continue to have greater strength. On that account it was decreed by the Edict of Moulins [1566] that rights of levying a direct tax (*droits de taille*), which lords pretended to have over their subjects, could not be enforced, notwithstanding the prescription of long time.

Yet this fact of long usage is the point at which judges and jurists have always **[246]** stopped, not permitting any inquiry as to whether the rights of sovereignty can be prescribed. For almost all of them are of the opinion that the rights of majesty can be acquired by passage of a period of time. It would be simpler to profess that these rights do not properly belong to a sovereign prince, which would be a capital crime, as they admit; otherwise they would have to say that the crown
{*530*} and sovereignty can be prescribed. Our judgment is the same with respect to exemptions from the payment of charges and impositions, which no one can grant unless he is sovereign. This too is abundantly spelled out in the Edict of Moulins. In this kingdom, an exemption has to be verified in the *Chambre des Comptes* and in the *Cour des Aides*.[33]

There is no reason to specify the cases in which a sovereign prince can impose a tax or subsidy on his subjects, if this power is his to the exclusion of all others.[34] Some have contended that the right of taxing salt is a more sovereign prerogative than any of the others. Nevertheless, in almost all commonwealths we find that many private individuals own salt pits, which can be part of the inheritance and property of private persons, as in ancient Rome. It is true that many sovereign princes, going back to ancient times, have laid a tax on salt, as did Lysimachus, king of Thrace; Ancus Martius, the king of the Romans (whose tax was increased by Livy the Censor, thenceforth surnamed the Salt-merchant [*le Saunier*, *Salinator*]); and Philip de Valois in this kingdom. But that does not prevent private individuals from owning salt-mines, as they would any other kind of mine, reserving for the prince his royalties and impositions.[35]

But rights to the sea belong solely to the sovereign prince, who can impose charges up to thirty leagues from his coast unless there is a
31} sovereign prince nearer by to prevent him, as was adjudged in a case involving the duke of Savoy.* And only a sovereign prince can grant a letter of safe-conduct, which the Italians call *guidage* {*guidagium*}, or exercise the right of wreckage, or *Warech*,[36] which is one of the articles included in the ordinance of the Emperor Frederick II **[247]**. This {barbaric right} was not claimed by sovereign princes in ancient times. But today the practice is common among all who have a seaport.† I remember having heard that the emperor's ambassador
2} brought complaints to the privy council of King Henry II in 1556 concerning the seizure by Giordano Orsini of two galleys that had been shipwrecked off Corsica. The constable replied that a wrecked ship is forfeited to the sovereign lord [of the coast], and that this is a general custom, not only in countries that obey the king, but in all the seas both east and west (*mais aussi en toute la mer du Levant et du Ponent*). It is also clear that Andrea‡ Doria lodged no complaint when the wrecks of two of his galleys were confiscated by the prior of Capua. We would have much the same to say of the duties that are levied merely for dropping anchor on a coast.§

Among the marks of sovereignty, many jurists include the seizure and appropriation of vacant properties such as [unclaimed] inheritances or lands, which are almost everywhere assigned to par-

*For "But rights to the sea . . . duke of Savoy" L170, D3–7 substitutes, "But since the ocean and the sea cannot be anybody's private property, it is recognized, as a kind of common right of all princes bordering the sea, that a prince has a jurisdiction over all persons approaching his coast up to sixty miles from the shore. And this was decided in a case involving the duke of Savoy."

†L171, A2–4 adds, "By what right, you ask? Error here creates the right. But if the misdeed is done knowingly rather than in error, it is a crime pretending to be error."

‡"Antonio" (Antoine) in the text, but corrected at L171, A9.

§L171, B1–2 adds, "although this [dropping of anchor] was once a right by the common law of peoples (*iuris gentium*)."

ticular [feudal] lords. Although by common law the Roman emperors customarily seized vacant properties and annexed them to the state domain, a private person could become the owner upon finding something that had been abandoned – for which we use the word
{533} *guerp*, and *deguerpir* for the verb. It is true that a sovereign prince had four years in which he could seize unclaimed inheritances. But in almost every part of Europe where feudal law is current, the lords take two thirds of ownerless movable property, with one third going to its finder, if the owner of the item does not present himself within forty days after public notification is given.*

We may say, consequently, that this right of the fisc (*droit de fisque*) is not a mark of sovereignty, since sovereign princes share it with all feudal lords having the power to administer justice (*tous seigneurs justiciers*). Indeed, even a sovereign prince has a treasury in his private capacity that is kept separate from that of the public, as well as his own private domain that has nothing in common with the public domain. The ancient Roman emperors thus kept each of these separate **[248]** and had different officers for each, a superintendent of the treasury, and a superintendent of the private inheritance (*patrimoine*).
{534} And King Louis XII, on coming to the throne, created the Chamber of Blois for his private domain of Blois, Montfort, and Coucy, apart from the duchy of Orléans which he already held as an appanage.†

Among these fiscal rights, however, there are some that belong only to the sovereign prince, such as the confiscation of estates for crimes of treason, with which heresy and counterfeiting are also included. In fact, there are some one hundred and fifty fiscal privileges, most of them proper only to a sovereign prince, which there is no need to take

*The sense of this paragraph is clearer in L171, B2–8, which substitutes, "Under Roman law, anyone was allowed to seize unoccupied or abandoned property. Now, however, only those who have power to command (*imperium*) or the administration of justice (*iurisdictio*) conceded to them by law or by custom can rightfully take possession of lost or abandoned property if it is not claimed by the owner within a certain interval of time, which in the case of movable property is set at forty days after public notice has been given. There was, to be sure, a four-year period set by the Roman emperors during which unoccupied possessions could be claimed by the prince. But at the end of four years, prescription ran against the treasury."

†L171, C2–5 is clearer, "Thus King Louis XII of France, when he obtained the scepter of this kingdom, ordered his private estates of Blois, Montfort, and Coucy divided from the duchy of Orleans and the rest of the public domain, and had their accounts kept separately." This discussion of the separation of public and private treasuries in kingdoms seems to digress from the main point, namely that the right of seizing vacant possessions is not a sovereign prerogative.

up one by one, since the jurists have already provided us with enough and perhaps too much in the way of subtleties about them. But the power of granting the right to hold a fair, which was a mark of sovereignty in ancient times, just as it is today, should be classified as a grant of privilege, and not included among fiscal prerogatives and various others like them that are touched upon above.*

As for the right of marque or reprisal, which sovereign princes [now] have to the exclusion of all others – in olden times it was not peculiar to them. Everyone was entitled to undertake reprisals without permission, either from a magistrate or from the prince, and this is
35} what the Latins called *clarigatio*.† But princes gradually gave this power to governors and magistrates, and in the end reserved it for their majesty in order to preserve the peace and give greater security to truces, which were often disrupted by reckless private individuals abusing their right of reprisal. In this kingdom, the Parlement used to grant letters of marque, as we see from a decree of 12 February 1392. But King Charles VIII expressly reserved that right in an edict of 1485.

As for the right of royalties (*droit des regales*), it is exclusive to the princes that make use of it. But since few of them claim this right, it ought not to be listed among the prerogatives of sovereignty,‡ any more than the formulae that princes put on their edicts, orders, and commissions, such as "By the grace of God," which King Louis XI forbade the duke of Brittany to use as his official formula. There are, however, many ancient treaties in the French treasury **[249]** in which the deputies sent to arrange a peace treaty or alliance style their offices as being "by the grace of God," including even a tax-collector who called himself "tax-collector of Meaux by the grace of God!"

*For "But the power of granting ... touched upon above" L171, D3–6 substitutes, "[And modern jurists] have confused the rights of majesty with fiscal rights and run the public together with the private. Thus the right to hold a fair, like all other privileges, is in the gift of the prince alone."

†L171, D8–L172, A2 supplies further details, "Anyone who had been harmed by the enemy could seize any of the enemy as a captive even in a time of truce. During wartime, moreover, anyone was allowed to take a captive even if no harm had been done him by the enemy."

‡L172, A10–B4 illustrates the right: "The French, furthermore, correctly speak of right of royalty (*ius regale*) when a prince, upon the death of a bishop, appropriates the latter's income until such time as a new bishop is elected by the chapter or appointed by the favor of the prince himself and has been put into possession of the office after taking his oath. But this is not universally practiced and should not be called a right of sovereignty."

And the kings of France have even reserved the right, from which feudal and judicial lords were all excluded, to use a seal of yellow wax. King Louis XI granted this as a special privilege to René of Anjou, king of Sicily, with the same privilege for his heirs, by letters patent of
{*536*} 18 July 1468, as verified in the Parlement; and this opened the way for Louis to obtain the county of Provence. A writer who used the *Mémoires* of Du Tillet for his book [on French public law] says "white wax," which our kings have never used, and is merely repeating that author's mistake.[37]

It would be more justified to say that compelling subjects to change their language is a mark of sovereignty. This is something that the Romans did so much better than any prince or people since, that they still seem to be dominant throughout the greater part of Europe. Yet the last king of the ancient Etruscans, after he was vanquished, gave the Romans everything they wanted but was utterly unwilling to accept the Latin tongue. As Cato says, *Latinas literas ut reciperet, persuaderi non potuit.** And since the Gauls had so many Roman citizens and colonies among them, they more or less changed the language of the country into something nearly Latin, which they called *Roman*, and issued all of their court decrees in Latin up until the ordinance of Francis I.† We also see how the Arabs have planted their language all over Asia and Africa, and how, just a few years ago, the king of Spain wanted to compel the Moors of Granada to change their dress and their language.

Among the marks of sovereignty, many have included the power to judge according to one's conscience. This is a power all judges have
{*537*} where there is no express law or custom; that is why, in edicts, one often sees in the articles left to the discretion of the judges, the clause, "With which we have charged their conscience." If there is a custom or ordinance in conflict [with his opinion], the judge has no power to go above the law or to dispute it. Indeed he was forbidden to do so by the laws of Lycurgus and by an ancient ordinance of Florence. But the prince can do this unless it is in express conflict with the law of God to which, we have shown, he remains subject.

[250] As for the title "majesty," it is clear enough that it belongs

* "He could not be persuaded to accept the Latin language."

† L172, D3–5 adds, "By a like edict, Edward III ordered the judges and magistrates of England to render their opinions in their native language rather than use French as before."

only to someone who is sovereign. Some rulers also take the title "sacred majesty," like the [German] emperor, others "excellent majesty," like the queen of England in her edicts and letters patent, although at one time emperors and kings did not use such titles.
38} Indeed the princes of Germany accord this title of "sacred majesty" to the kings of France as well as to the emperor; and I have seen letters written by the princes of the Empire to the king for the release of Count Mansfield, then a prisoner in France, in which the letters "VSM" – that is, "your sacred majesty" – appear six times, which is a title proper to God to the exclusion of all human princes. Other, non-sovereign, princes use the word "highness," like the dukes of Lorraine, Savoy, Mantua, Ferrara, and Florence; or "excellence," like the princes of the *pays de surceance* [in Burgundy], or else "serenity" like the dukes of Venice.

Here I am omitting many petty rights on which sovereign princes insist in one or another country, but which are in no way marks of sovereignty. For the latter are proper to all sovereign princes to the exclusion of all other lords having administration of justice, magistrates, and subjects; and by their very nature they are untransferable, inalienable, and imprescriptible. Whatever gift of land or lordship a sovereign prince may make, the royal rights inherent in his majesty are always reserved, even if they were not spelled out explicitly. So was it decided for the appanages of France by an ancient decree of the court; they cannot be prescribed or usurped by any period of time no matter what its length. For if the public lands of the commonwealth cannot be acquired by prescription, how, then, the rights and prerogatives of sovereignty? Yet it is indubitable, from all the edicts and ordinances concerning them, that public lands are inalienable, and cannot be acquired by the passage of a period of time.
9} Nor is this a novel rule of law, since more than two thousand years ago Themistocles, moving to recapture public land usurped by private individuals, said in the speech he made to the people of Athens, "Men cannot prescribe against God, or private individuals against the commonwealth." And Cato the Censor used the same maxim in an oration delivered to the Roman people for **[251]** the reintegration of public land usurped by certain private individuals. How, then, could the rights and prerogatives of sovereignty be prescribed? This is why anyone who employs the prerogatives reserved to the sovereign prince is guilty in law of a capital offense.

So much then concerning the principal points of sovereign majesty, on which I have been as brief as possible, having treated this subject more amply in my book, *De imperio*.[38] And since the form and state of a commonwealth depend on who holds the sovereignty, let us see how many sorts of commonwealth there are.

3} BOOK II, CHAPTER I

Of the kinds of state in general and whether there are more than three

Now that we have spoken of sovereignty, and of the rights and marks thereof, we have to see, in any given commonwealth, who has sovereignty in order to determine what its state is. If sovereignty lies in a single prince, we will call it monarchy; if all of the people have a share, we will say that the state is democratic (*populaire*); if it is only the lesser part of the people, we will hold that the state **[252]** is aristocratic. We will employ [only] these terms in order to avoid the confusion and obscurity arising from the variety of good or bad rulers which has prompted many to distinguish more than three kinds of state. For if that opinion prevailed, and the state of a commonwealth were determined by some standard of virtue or vice, there would be a world of them. But it is clear that to have true definitions and resolutions in any subject matter, one must fix not on accidents, which are
4} innumerable, but on essential differences of form. Otherwise one could fall into an infinite labyrinth which does not admit of scientific knowledge. One would be coining types of state not only from the whole range of virtues and vices, but also from things that are morally indifferent, such as whether the monarch was chosen for his strength, or for his good looks, or for his height, or for his nobility [of birth], or for his wealth, which are all indifferent things. Or one could ask whether he was chosen king for being the most warlike, or the most peaceable, or the wisest, or the most just, or the most magnificent, or the most learned, or the soberest, or the humblest, or the simplest, or the most chaste; and so, going on this way with all the other qualities, one would arrive at an infinity of monarchies. And the same would be true of the aristocratic state, depending on whether the lesser part of

the people held sovereignty as the richest, or the noblest, or the wisest, or the most just, or the most warlike; or held for a corresponding range of vices or other [morally] indifferent qualities – which is absurd. Hence the opinion that gives rise to such absurdity should be rejected.

Since, therefore, an [accidental] quality does not alter the [essential] nature of things, we shall say that there are only three states, or three kinds, of commonwealth – monarchy, aristocracy, and democracy. The term "monarchy," as we have said, applies when a single individual has the sovereignty and the rest of the people have only to look on; a "democracy," or popular state, when the whole people, or the greater part thereof, have sovereign power as a body; an "aristocracy," when the lesser part of the people has sovereignty as a body and gives law to the rest of the people both collectively and individually.

The ancients all agreed that there were three forms at a minimum; but some added a **[253]** fourth compounded of these three. Plato, to be sure, added a fourth form in which the good were sovereign, which properly speaking is a pure aristocracy, but did not accept the mixture
{*545*} of the three [basic types] as a form of state.* Aristotle accepted Plato's [additional form] and also the mixture of the basic three,† and thus arrives at five forms. Polybius‡ has seven forms – three commendable, three perverted, and one compounded of the first three. Dionysius of Halicarnassus,§ along with Polybius' first three, has a fourth compounded of those three, and around the same time Cicero and, after him, Thomas More in his *Utopia*, Contarini, Machiavelli, and many other authors have held the same opinion. This opinion, however, is very old, and does not begin with Polybius, who nevertheless gets credit for it, or with Aristotle, because four hundred years earlier it was brought to light by Herodotus, who said that many took it for the best form of state, even though he holds that there are only three and that all the others are imperfect.

*For "Plato . . . form of state" L175, B3–5 substitutes, "Plato constructs a fourth type by mixing not three but two – that is, tyranny and democracy – or by constructing the rule of the best – that is, of those who excel all the rest in virtue." (The first part of this sentence appears to be an allusion to Plato's best state in the *Laws*, the second to the ideal state of the *Republic*.)

†Bodin note: *Politics*, Book IV, par. 7.

‡Bodin note: *Histories*, Book VI.

§Bodin note: *Roman Antiquities*, Book II, pars. 7, 14.

And were it not that reason has forced me to maintain the contrary, the authority of such great figures might have overwhelmed me. Strong reasons must be given, therefore, to show that their opinion is mistaken, and that is best accomplished by refuting their own reasonings and examples. They state it as a fact that the Spartan, Roman, and Venetian states were compounds in which royal, aristocratic, and democratic power were subtly blended with each other. Indeed, when Plato wrote that the best form of state was a compound of democracy and tyranny,[1] he was abruptly repudiated by his disciple Aristotle, who 46} said that nothing solid could come of that, and that it is better to construct a state compounded of all three together. Here, however Aristotle contradicts himself. For if the mixture of two states is bad – that is, the mixture of two extremes (which, in every other domain, combine to form a mean) – the mixture of three would be even worse. And inasmuch as this notion [of a mixed state] can incite great troubles in commonwealths and have extraordinary consequences, it has to be examined closely. For when states are contrary to each other, as are monarchy and democracy, contrary laws and ordinances must be established in consideration of the form of state.

The wisest and best informed citizens of Florence had accepted **[254]** the opinion of the ancients and believed that the best state was a mixture of the three basic forms. When it was decided, on the advice of Pier Soderini, to give control of the state to the people, they did not want the dregs of the commons to have a share of sovereignty, but only the [descendants of the] oldest houses, as they called the residents of the first and second circles of the town walls, and the richest class of citizens. They would not [even] allow the great council of those who were to share in sovereignty to have cognizance of all the state's affairs, but only the power to make laws, create officers, and dispose of the resources of the public treasury; everything else was to be managed by the privy council and the magistrates. This they thought was to mix the three kinds of state. But if a single state could thus be compounded of all three, it would surely have to be wholly different from any one of them, just as we can see that the harmonic proportion, which is composed of the arithmetic and geometric, is entirely different from either of these.[2] The same holds for the mixture of natural substances, where the combination of two simple 47} elements has a special virtue of its own completely different from the simple elements of which it is composed. But the mixture of the three basic forms of state does not produce a different kind. The combination of royal, aristocratic, and democratic power makes only a democracy.[3]

This outcome might appear to be avoided if sovereignty were given to the monarch on day one, and the lesser part of the people had power on the day following, and after that the entire people. Each one of the three would thus have its turn at being sovereign, just as the senators of [early] Rome, on the death of a king, had sovereign power for a certain number of days, each one in turn. Yet even so, there would be only three kinds of state. And they would not last long, any more than a badly organized household where the wife commands the husand as the head and then each of the servants in succession.

But [really] to combine monarchy with democracy and with aristocracy is impossible and contradictory, and cannot even be imagined. For if sovereignty is indivisible, as we have shown, how could it be shared by a prince, the nobles, and the people at the same time? The first prerogative of sovereignty is to give the law to **[255]** subjects. But who will be the subjects and who will obey if they also have the power to make law? And who will be able to make a law if he is himself constrained to receive it from those to whom he gives it? But if no one in particular has the power to make law, and the power resides in all together, then it follows of necessity that the state is democratic.* Or if we give the people power to make the laws and create the officers, and forbid it to meddle in the rest, we would still have to admit that the power granted to the officers belongs to the people, and is conceded to the magistrates only as a trust, which the people is as much entitled to end as to create, so that the state will always be democratic.

To verify what I have said, let us take the very examples that Polybius, Contarini, and others have left us. They say that the Spartan
{548} state was compounded of three because there were two kings, the senate of twenty-eight which embodied aristocracy, and the five ephors which represented democracy. But how would they answer

*"But who will be the subjects ... state is democratic." L176, C11–D4 comes to a conclusion more consistent with the premises of Bodin's example: "But what citizens would allow themselves to be bound by a command against their will if they at the same time had the power to coerce its maker? Indeed if they do obey willingly, their own sovereignty is lost. But if both parties refuse to take commands, and no one obeys or commands, it will be not commonwealth but anarchy, which is worse than the cruelest tyranny."

Herodotus, who uses the Spartan state as an example of pure aristocracy? And how would they respond to Thucydides, Xenophon, Aristotle, and Plutarch? Writing of the Peloponnesian War (which lasted for twenty-one years as a war between democratic and aristocratic commonwealths), they say the sole aim of the Athenians and their allies was to change aristocracies into democracies as they did in Samos, Corfu, and all the other cities that they subjected; while the intention of the Spartans, to the contrary, was to change democracies into aristocracies, which is what in fact they did in all the cities of Greece after Lysander's victory, including the city of Athens itself, where they took sovereignty away from the people and gave it, in the Spartan form and manner, to thirty aristocrats who were called the thirty tyrants. In the cities of Samos, Sicyon, Aegina, Melos, and other cities of Asia Minor, they gave sovereignty to ten lords and a captain, recalled the exiles who had stood for aristocracy, and banished the chiefs of the democratic parties. And, finally, what would these proponents of mixture say to Maximus of Tyre, who takes Sparta as the prime example of an aristocratic regime **[256]**, followed by Thessaly, Pella, Crete, and Mantinea? They would have to prove that all these authors were lying, since they lived in the very places and for the most part in the very times in which the Athenian and Spartan commonwealths flourished. But they are surely more believable than a Florentine, a Venetian, or an Englishman.[4]

What led Polybius and Contarini astray perhaps* is the title "kings" which Lycurgus let remain with the two nobles of the house of Hercules after he had taken away their power and with their own
9} agreement and consent given it to the people. It is no doubt true that their power had already been shaken. Ever since the time that King Aristodemus, who was a sovereign prince in Sparta, left two children who succeeded to the throne together (as did Amphareus and Leucippus among the Messenians), there were two kings ruling conjointly, such that neither the one nor the other was king and they often obstructed each other out of jealousy. The outcome was that they were finally stripped of their sovereignty by Lycurgus, who was also a prince of the blood; although the royal name remained in their house, they had no more power than the other twenty-eight nobles. This is much like what happened at Athens and Rome after the kings were

*L177, C3–4 clarifies this, "What, then, misled Polybius who was, after all, a citizen of Megalopolis which is very near to Sparta?"

expelled. They left the name of king to a priest whom they called the king of sacrifices because he was charged with performing certain sacrifices which the king alone used to perform before. But even then he was subject to the high priest, and he cold not, as Plutarch tells us, have any office or magistracy, something which was possible for all the other priests. The same was done by Lycurgus with the two kings of Sparta, who were no more than senators, having only the right to vote without any power of command. On the contrary, they were required to obey the orders of the ephors, who often condemned them to monetary fines, and sometimes even to death, as they did kings Agis and Pausanias. Hence sovereignty lay in the people who had full power to confirm or invalidate the decrees and counsels of the senate. Thucydides, furthermore, refutes the error of those who thought that the kings had two votes each.

But a hundred years later the state as Lycurgus had reformed it was altered by kings Polydorus and Theopompus because the people were difficult to assemble, and too often reversed the most solemn decrees
{*550*} of the senate. They changed **[257]** the democratic state into an aristocracy by craftily exploiting an oracle of Apollo which they twisted to support the project. It was inferred from the oracle that the Senate of the Thirty should henceforth be all-powerful in affairs of state, so that the senators became sovereign lords. To appease the people and make it forget what was being taken from it, the kings proposed that the five ephors, who were chosen from the people, should act like tribunes for the purpose of preventing tyranny.* Every nine years, in fact, the ephors scanned a clear sky and if they saw a shooting star, says Plutarch, they put their kings in prison and did not let them out until the oracle of Apollo said they should. This is what was done with the king of Cuma by the phylactes, or jailer, who put him in prison every year and did not let him out until the senate ordered it, as we read in [Plutarch's] *Aphorisms of the Greeks*. The Spartan state lasted thus for five hundred years until the time of Cleomenes, who killed the ephors and removed power from the thirty nobles. Although Antigonus, king of Macedonia, took over the state

*"To appease the people . . . preventing tyranny." L178, A10–B4 elaborates and modifies this, "That the people should not grieve for the power taken from it, it was decided that five ephors taken from the commoners should be created who would examine the statements, acts, and projects of the kings and do anything they had to do in order to prevent them from slipping into tyranny." (The Latin makes it clear that the ephors could control the kings but, unlike the tribunes at Rome, could not control the Senate.)

after defeating Cleomenes and quickly restored it to what it had been before, twenty years afterwards it fell into the hands of Nabis the tyrant. After he was killed by Philopomen, the commonwealth was annexed to the Achaen state until it was liberated by the Romans thirty years later.

This in a few words is the true history of the Spartan state, which Plutarch put together by going through all the local archives. It is a story that had not been properly understood before – not by Plato, nor by Aristotle, nor by Polybius, nor by Xenophon; and that is the reason why many commentators mistakenly thought that it was a mixture of
51} the three forms of state. The reality is evident from the reply that Nabis the First, tyrant of Sparta, gave to Q. Flaminius: *Noster legumlator Lycurgus, non in paucorum manu rempublicam esse voluit, quem vos senatum appellatis, ne eminere unum aut alterum ordinem in civitate, sed per aequationem fortunae ac dignitatis fore credidit, ut multi essent, qui pro patria arma ferrent.** Even though he was trying to disguise a tyranny that was completely contrary to what he said, he was nevertheless telling the truth as to what Lycurgus had done. But let us go on.

The partisans of the mixed constitution have also **[258]** adduced the Roman state as an example, which they say was a mixture of the royal, democratic, and aristocratic states. The proof thereof, says Polybius, is that one sees royal power in the consuls, aristocracy in the Senate, and democracy in the Estates of the people. Dionysius of Halicarnassus, Cicero, Contarini, and various others have followed this opinion, which is nonetheless implausible. In the first place, royal power cannot exist in two individuals; monarchy, being something unified in its very nature, can never have an associate, or else, as we have shown, it is a kingdom and a monarchy no longer. Indeed, it would make better sense to attribute the status of a monarch to the duke of Genoa or the doge of Venice. And what royal power could there have been in two consuls who had no power to make law, or peace, or war, or to create a magistrate, to grant a pardon, to spend a single penny of the public treasury, or even to condemn a citizen to be whipped unless in time of war? Since this last was always given to every captain-in-chief, they too would have to be called kings, and with more plausibility than the consuls who held power only by turns

* "Our lawgiver, Lycurgus, did not want the commonwealth to be in the hands of a few, which you call a senate, nor did he want one or the other order to stand higher in the citizen body, but believed that by equalizing fortunes and honors there would be a large number of people who would bear arms for their country."

and for a year.* The constable in this kingdom, the first pasha in
{552} Turkey,† the bethudeta in Ethiopia, and the edegnar in the kingdoms of Africa have ten times more power than the two consuls together, and yet they are the slaves and subjects of their princes, just as the consuls were the servants and subjects of the people. And how can anyone say that the consuls had royal authority in view of the fact that the least tribune of the people could throw them into prison? Thus the tribune Drusus had the consul Philippus seized by the collar and thrown into prison for interrupting his speech to the people.

The power of the consuls was to lead the armies, to convene the Senate, to receive the letters of captains and allies and transmit them to the Senate, to provide ambassadors with an audience before the people or the Senate, to convene the great Estates [*comitia centuriata*], and to ask the opinion of the people on the creation of officers or publication of laws. Yet they always remained standing as they spoke, with their maces (*masses*, *fasces*) lowered to indicate subjection, as they faced the people who were seated. In the absence of the consuls, furthermore, the highest magistrate who was present at Rome had the same power. In addition, the consuls had power only for a year. But I shall pass over **[259]** the opinion [that the consuls were royal] since it is hardly worth refuting.

As for the Senate, which they say had a species of aristocratic power, it had so little that almost every privy council[5] that ever existed had more. It had no power of issuing commands either to private individuals or to magistrates, and could not even assemble legitimately unless at the pleasure of the consuls. During the year of his consulate, Caesar assembled the Senate only once or twice, and went to the people for everything he wanted; and it was not at all
{553} uncommon for the consul to act as he pleased, against the Senate's advice. Even when the authority {*auctoritas*} of the Senate was at its highest point ever, the consuls, so we read, refused to act when the Senate, finding a public emergency, petitioned them to name a dictator. The Senate, without the power to command and having neither sergeant nor lictor, which are the true marks of those having power to

*For "Since this last ... and for a year" L179, A8–B1 substitutes, "As for Polybius' point, that consuls had the power of capital punishment (*gladii ius*) over soldiers, it is no wonder, since this right is and always has been shared by praetors, military tribunes, and every legion commander in order to maintain military discipline. In addition, the consuls had power only for a year and on alternate days."

†"the first pasha in Turkey" is omitted at L179, B3.

command, sent Servilius Priscus, the senator, to appeal to the tribunes thus: "*Vos Tribuniplebis Senatus appellat, ut in tanto discrimine reipublicae Dictatorem dicere Consules pro vestra potestate cogatis.*" *Tribuni pro collegio pronunciant, placere Consules Senatus dicto audientes esse, aut in vincula se duci iussoros.** At another place [in Livy] it is reported that the Senate was of the opinion that the consuls should ask the people to name a person of its choice as dictator and that, if the consul was unwilling to do so, the urban praetor should make the request, and *si ne is quidem vellet, Tribuniplebis: Consul negavit se populum rogaturum, Praetorem rogare vetuit: Tribuniplebis rogarunt.*† It is thus evident that the Senate lacked the power of issuing commands even to lesser magistrates if a higher magistrate forbade it.

As for Polybius' statement that the Senate had the power of bringing cities and provinces to judgment before it, and of punishing conspirators against the state, there is clear evidence to the contrary in Livy. When the question arose in the Senate as to punishing the Capuan {Campanian} traitors who had allied themselves with Hannibal after the battle of Cannae, a venerable senator said in open session, *Per Senatum agi de Campanis iniussu non video posse*‡ and, a little further on, *ut rogatio feratur ad populum, qua Senatui potestas fiat statuendi de Campanis.*§ And when a proposal to this end was presented to **[260]** the people, it gave the Senate its commission and order
54} to try the Capuans, saying *Quod Senatus maxima pars censeat, qui assident id volumus iubemusque.*¶

Polybius was also mistaken in saying that the Senate disposed of the provinces and their governments at its pleasure, since Livy says in Book 28 that *Q. Fulvius postulavit a Consule, ut palam in Senatu diceret, permitteretne Senatui, ut de provinciiis , staturusque eo esset quod censuisset, an ad populum laturus: Scipio respondit, se quod e Republica esset facturum.*

*" 'Tribunes of the people, the Senate calls upon you in this time of great danger to the commonwealth to invoke your power and compel the consuls to appoint a dictator.' The tribunes, speaking as a body, declared that the consuls would pay heed to the Senate's request or they would have them led away in chains."

†"if he too was unwilling, then the tribunes. The consul said he would not ask the people; the praetor he forbade to ask; and so the tribunes asked it."

‡"I do not see how the Senate can act on the Campanians without an order from the people."

§"Let a proposal be put before the people by which the Senate would be empowered to decide on the Campanians."

¶"Our will and our command is whatever the majority of those present in the Senate shall decide."

*Tum Fluvius, a vobis peto Tribuniplebes, ut mihi auxilio sitis.** This makes it very clear that the Senate had no power except by sufferance of the tribunes and the people. And he who has nothing but by sufferance, as we said above, does not have anything at all. To sum it up: there is no decision on affairs of state, and especially no advice or decision of the Senate, that had any force or strength whatsoever if the people did not order it, or the tribunes of the people did not consent to it. This is something that we have touched upon above and which we will treat more elaborately in our chapter on the Senate.

There is thus no doubt whatever that, after the expulsion of the kings, the Roman state was democratic except for a period of two years when the ten commissioners {*decemviri*}, created to reform the customs, changed the democracy into an aristocracy – or, to put it more accurately, into an oligarchy, which was then overthrown by a conspiracy. I said above that the power of magistrates, no matter how great it might be, does not belong to them and that they have it only in trust. Well, it is certain that at the beginning the people elected the senators and then, to relieve themselves of the trouble, gave a commission for this purpose to the censors, who were also elected by the people, so that the entire authority of the Senate was held of the
{*555*} people (*dependoit du peuple*), which was accustomed to confirm or disallow, ratify or set aside the decrees of the Senate at its pleasure.

Contarini passed the same judgment on the Venetian state, saying that it is a mixture of the three forms of state just like Rome and Sparta. For the royal power, he says, is in the duke of Venice, the aristocratic in the senate, and the democratic in the Great Council. Since then, however, Giannotti has cast light on the true state of the Venetian commonwealth and has given clear evidence, drawn from the ancient archives of Venice, that [261] Contarini was very much mistaken. Giannotti shows that the Venetian state was a pure monarchy only during the three hundred years previous to Sebastian Ciano's becoming duke, whereas Contarini holds that it was established as we now find it eight hundred years ago, and Paolo Manuzio says twelve hundred years. However this may be, it is certain that at present it is a true aristocracy. For of the fifty-nine thousand

*"Q. Fulvius demanded that the consul say openly in the Senate whether he would permit the Senate to decide as to the provinces and stand by its determination, or whether he would take it to the people. Scipio replied that he would do what was best for the state. Fulvius then said, 'I appeal to you, tribunes, for support.'"

three hundred and forty-nine Venetians who were counted twenty years ago (not including children under the age of six or those who ranked as gentlemen of Venice), it was only [these] four or five thousand gentlemen, young and old, who had a share in public life. Of this number, clerics and youths under twenty-five years of age were only onlookers and could not enter the Great Council, except that some juniors, who requested it, might be admitted at the age of twenty if they seemed to be more mature in judgment than the others. For a hundred years the Great Council, assembled to decide on important affairs, has not numbered more than fifteen hundred, with all the rest left out, as one can see from the histories of Sabellico and
56} Cardinal Bembo. Sovereignty thus lies in a minority of the Venetians belonging to a particular group of noble families. For not all native-born gentlemen of Venice are admitted; among those of the same stock, the same race, the same name, some are citizens who do not attend the Great Council, while others do. I will not give the reason for this here since anyone can find it in Sabellico.*

The Great Council, says Contarini, has sovereign power to make and repeal laws, to install and remove all officers, to take appeals in the last resort, to decide on peace and war, and to pardon the condemned. Contarini thus contradicts himself. For if things are as he says, no one can deny that sovereignty in that commonwealth is aristocratic. It would be so, indeed, even if the Great Council had no other power than† the right of creating officers. For whatever power the officers have, they hold of the ruling body, which suffices to show that the [council of] Ten, the Senate, the [council of the] Wise, and the duke with his six counsellors have power only on sufferance and only for as long as it pleases the Great Council. As for the duke, Contarini himself admits that he does not [even] have the power to summon anyone **[262]** before him, which is the most basic prerogative of the power to command and is given to the lowest magistrates. The duke, furthermore, can make no decision having to do with public affairs or justice except in the assembly of his six counsellors, or of the Ten, the Wise, the senate, the forty judges for civil or criminal cases, or the Great Council. Although he has entrée to all the guilds and corporations, he has only one vote like any other member; and he

*"For not all native born . . . Sabellico" is omitted, perhaps because repetitious, at L181, A8.

†L181, B1–2 adds, "the law-making power and."

dares not open any letter addressed to the government except in the presence of the six counsellors or the Ten, nor does he dare to leave the city {without authorization}. The duke Marin Faliero was even hanged for having married a foreign woman without the advice of the
{557} council, and twelve other dukes of Venice were put to death for abusing their power, as one can read in Sabellico. Yet the duke wears a rich headcovering and a robe made of cloth of gold; he is attended, honored, and respected like a prince; and the coinage bears his name (although it carries the corporation's stamp). All these things, I conceded, suggest the status of a prince. But in practice, the duke has nothing in the way of power or right to command.

But if we were thus to judge the state of commonwealths by clothes and outward show, there would be none that was not mixed the way they say. Thus the German Empire would be much more of a mixture than Venice. The emperor has even more numerous and more significant prerogatives than the duke of Venice; the seven prince electors, together with the other princes, are a semblance of aristocracy or oligarchy; and the ambassadors of the imperial cities resemble a democracy. Nevertheless, it is quite certain that the state of the German Empire is a pure aristocracy composed of three or four hundred persons at the most, as we have explained above. The Swiss would also hold that their state is a mixture of the three regimes, the council exhibiting an aristocratic regime; the *avoyer*, or burgomaster, representing the royal state; and the general and local assemblies the democratic state. Nevertheless, it is well known that all their commonwealths are either aristocracies or democracies.

Some have even dared to voice and print the opinion that the French state too is compounded of the three types of commonwealth – the Parlement of Paris embodying a form of aristocracy, the Three Estates embodying democracy, and the king representing **[263]** the royal state – an opinion which is not only absurd but punishable by death.[6] For it is *lèse majesté* to make subjects the colleagues of a sovereign prince. What semblance of a democracy is there in the
{558} assembly of the Three Estates, where each individually and all collectively bend the knee and present humble requests and petitions, which the king accepts or rejects just as he sees fit? And what democratic counterweight against the monarch's majesty can there be in the assembly of the Three Estates – or indeed in the whole people

if it could be assembled in one place – which requests, petitions, and reveres its king? So far is such an assembly from diminishing the power of a sovereign prince that his majesty is much augmented and exalted by it. He cannot be elevated to a higher degree of honor, power, and glory than to see an infinite number of princes and great lords, and an innumerable populace of all sorts and human conditions, throwing themselves at his feet and paying homage to his majesty. For the honor, glory, and power of princes lie only in the obedience, homage, and service of their subjects.

There is thus not a shadow of democratic power in the assembly of the Three Estates as it exists in this kingdom, its function being no more and even less than in Spain and England. Much less is there any suggestion of aristocracy either in the court of peers or in the assembly of all the kingdom's officers,[7] considering, above all, that the presence of the king causes the cessation of the power and authority of all corporations and guilds, and of all officials generally and individually, such that there is not a single magistrate who has power to command when he is present, as we shall explain in due course. With the king seated on his throne of justice, the chancellor turns to him first of all to learn his pleasure, and the king then orders the chancellor to gather the counsel and opinion of the princes of the blood and of the great lords, peers, and magistrates. This is not so that judgment may be given by majority vote,* but only to acquaint the king with their counsel, which he may accept or reject at his pleasure. Most often he follows the opinion of the majority. But to make it understood that he did not have to, **[264]** the chancellor, in announcing the decree, does not say "the council or the court says," but rather, "the king says unto you."

We also see that the court of Parlement, when writing to the king, still preserves the ancient form. At the heading of such letters we read "To our sovereign lord, the king"; at the beinning "Our sovereign lord! With all possible humility we commend ourselves to your good
59} grace"; and in signing at the very end, "Your most humble and obedient subjects and servants, the people holding your court of Parlement." This is the speech not of aristocratic lords or colleagues in authority, but of true and humble subjects. But since I have

*L182, C5 adds, "as is done in judicial panels."

touched on this point above, I pass over it somewhat lightly here. France, then, is a pure monarchy unmixed with democratic power and still less with aristocracy.

Indeed, such mixture is completely impossible and contradictory. Aristotle, examining that opinion more closely in Book IV, chapter 8 of his *Politics*, indeed says that the term *politeia*, or commonwealth, is used for a system that is compounded of aristocracy and democracy. But he does not say how this could be accomplished and does not give an example.[8] On the contrary, in the tenth chapter of the same book,[9] he admits that none existed in his time and that he had not found any that had existed earlier, even though he is said to have collected one hundred constitutions in a book that has been lost. On the other hand, he does say that Plato's state[10] was neither aristocratic nor democratic but a third form compounded of the two, for which he uses the generic name "commonwealth" [*politeia*], as I have said. Aristotle, however, never reported Plato's true opinions. On the contrary, he invariably disguised them, as the members of the Academy very rightly noted. This is especially true when he was attacking Plato's *Republic*, so that many who rely on what Aristotle said have been very seriously misled. Hence I shall take just a word or two to present Plato's true opinion, which deserves to be understood since it helps us to comprehend the present question, to which one must add that some take his opinion as divine and others tread it under foot before they have even read it.

Plato constructed two states, the first of which he attributes to Socrates, **[265]** who, says Xenophon, never had the thoughts that Plato puts into his mouth. In the first of these states, he removes the
{*560*} words "mine" and "thine" as being the source of all evil, and would have all goods, women, and children held in common. But seeing how widely he was criticized for this, he quietly pulled back from it, as though he had written it only for purposes of discussion rather than to put it into practice. The second state, which is the one attributed to Plato, removes the community of goods, women, and children. For the rest, the two states are similar. In either of them Plato wants there to be no more than five thousand and forty citizens, a number that he chose because it had fifty-nine divisors (*parties entières, divisores*). He then divides them into three estates – the guardians, the warriors, and the workers – and introduces three classes of citizens, which are unequal in property. As for sovereignty, he assigns it to the assembly

of the entire people, for he gives the people as a whole the power of making and repealing law. This would be sufficient to conclude that the state is democratic, even if there were nothing else. But he goes on to give the assembly of the whole people the power of installing and removing all the officers and, not content with that, he also wants the people to have full power to judge all criminal cases since all the people, he says, have an interest therein. In short, he gives the people the power of life and death, of passing condemnations, and of granting pardons, all of which are clear indications of a democratic state. For there is no sovereign magistrate who represents the royal state; and there is no form of aristocracy, since he would have the senate, or the council on affairs of state which he calls the guardians, composed of four hundred citizens elected at the pleasure of the people. This clearly shows that Plato's state is the most democratic ever, and more so even than his native Athens, which is said to have been the most democratic state in all the world. I am leaving out the seven hundred and twenty-six laws that he set down for the governance of his com-
61} monwealth, since it suffices for my purpose to have shown that, with respect to the form of the state, Aristotle, Cicero, Contarini, and many others were mistaken in holding that Plato's state was tempered and compounded out of the three forms, or at least of aristocracy and democracy.*

We **[266]** shall conclude, then, that there is not now, and never was, a state compounded of aristocracy and democracy, much less of the three forms of state, but that there are only three kinds of state.† Herodotus was the first to say this, and Tacitus, who put it even better, said, *Cunctas nationes et urbes populius, aut primores, aut singuli regunt.*‡

Someone may object, however, that it might be possible to construct a state wherein the people creates the officers, disposes of expenditures, and grants pardons – which are three prerogatives of

*"Aristotle, Cicero, Contarini . . . aristocracy and democracy." L183, D6–9 lays special blame on Aristotle, "Plato's imagined state was not compounded of aristocracy and democracy as Aristotle claimed; Cicero, Contarini, and others in their turn took over his error, and led the rest, albeit in good faith, to make the same mistake."

†". . . but that there are only three kinds of state." L183, D11–12 is significantly more emphatic, "and [a mixture] cannot even be imagined, but only the three basic forms are possible (*at ne opinione quidem fingi, sed tria tantum genera constitui posse*)."

‡"All nations and cities are ruled either by the people, or the nobles, or single individuals."

sovereignty; where the nobility makes the laws, decides on peace and war, and levies duties and taxes – which are also prerogatives of sovereignty; and where there exists in addition a royal magistrate above all others to whom the people as a whole and each person in particular renders fealty and homage, and who judges in the last resort without there being any means of appealing from his decision or presenting a civil request (*requeste civile*) [for a re-hearing]. This, apparently, would be a way of dividing the rights and marks of sovereignty and composing a state that was aristocratic, royal, and democratic all at once. But I answer that no such state has ever existed and that none can be made or even imagined, because the prerogatives of sovereignty are indivisible. For the part that has the power to make law for everyone – that is, to command or forbid whatever it pleases without anyone being able to appeal from, or even to oppose, its commands – that part, I say, will forbid the others to make peace or war, to levy taxes, or to render fealty and homage without its leave; and he to whom fealty and liege homage is due will obligate the nobility and the people to render obedience to no one but
{562} himself. Hence it must always come to arms until such time as sovereignty resides in a prince, in the lesser part of the people, or in all the people.*

As an example, we can see how the Danish nobility ever since the time of Christian, the great-grandfather of the present King Frederick, has attempted to subject their kings. After conspiring against King Christian, they drove him from his throne, and put his cousin in possession on condition that he would not decide war or peace without permission from the senate, and would have no power {without the senate} to inflict the death penalty on any gentleman, along with many other restrictions of a similar sort which I shall set down in due course. From that time forth, the kings have sworn to observe these restrictions; and to make sure **[267]** that they do not break them, the nobility prevents the king from concluding any lasting

*"Hence it must always come to arms . . . all the people." L184, B6–C1 is more expansive, "And as each part will vigorously defend its own rights without yielding the rights it has assumed, this arrangement will be at odds with the nature of authority, in that the same person who has a supreme power of command will be compelled to obey someone else who is his subject. This makes it clear that, where the rights of sovereignty are divided between a prince and his subjects, a state of confusion must result in which the issue of ultimate control will be decided by force of arms until supreme power is in one man, in a few, or in the entire body of citizens."

peace (*ne veut pas qu'il face la paix*) and has formed an alliance against the king with the king of Poland and the rulers of Lubeck for the protection of their liberty. As a result, we might say that the king of Denmark and his nobility each have a share of sovereignty. But one can also say that this commonwealth has no assured repose, any more than had the king of Sweden, who so distrusted the nobility that he had a German as his chancellor and a Norman gentleman named Varennes as his constable.*

Mixture, then, is not a state, but rather the corruption of a state. Hence Herodotus said that there are but three forms of commonwealth, and that the others are corruptions which are continually agitated by the storms of civil sedition until sovereignty is wholly lodged in one form or another.

It might still be objected that at Rome the lesser part of the people, chosen from the very rich, made the laws, elected the highest magistrates – that is, the consuls, praetors, and censors – had the sovereign power of life and death, and disposed of all matters having to do with
63} war; that the majority of the people as a whole elected the lesser magistrates – namely, the ten tribunes of the people, the twenty-four military tribunes, the two aediles or *eschevins*, the treasurers, the officers of the guard and of coinage – and bestowed all vacant benefices; and that the majority of the people prior to Sulla adjudicated high criminal proceedings if they did not involve the penalty of natural or civil death. By this arrangement, it might be argued, the state was compounded of aristocracy and democracy, which is what the ancients called commonwealth [*politeia*, *respublica*] in the strictest sense.

I grant that there is some semblance of truth in this, but I would still reply that the state was a proper democracy. It is true that the great Estates of the people [*comitia centuriata*] were divided into six classes according to personal wealth; that the equestrians,[11] the majority of the senators and nobility, and the wealthiest segment of the people were all in the first class; and that, if just this class was agreed, a law that had been proposed was published and high magistrates that had stood for election were summoned to the estates

*"... king of Sweden ... constable." L184, D1–6 elaborates, "The government of Sweden is tossed about by the same kind of storms and heavy seas. The king used to live in such fear of his nobility that King Henry had a French constable and a German chancellor, and yet he was finally driven from his throne and palace by the nobility and put in prison where he has now languished for seventeen years."

to take their oath. It is also true that the five remaining classes had ten times more citizens, and in the event that the centuries in the first class did not all agree, the second was consulted, **[268]** and so on down to the sixth and last class, which contained the dregs of the people.[12] It is true that it did not often get to them. Yet to hold that the state was democratic, it suffices that all the people had a share, even though the rich and the noble were consulted first. Even so, the ordinary people – that is, the great majority of the people not including the nobility – seeing that its right to vote was vain, rose in so many revolts in a span of less than twenty or thirty years after the kings were expelled, that it obtained the power to make law, to decide on peace and war, and to ratify or annul everything that was recommended by the Senate, as we have already said above. And it passed an ordinance
{*564*} that the nobility should not attend the assemblies of the common people, which is an indisputable argument for holding that the state was one of the most democratic that ever existed. For once the common people obtained the advantage of being able to make law,[13] the *comitia centuriata* (*grands estats*) made no more than a dozen laws in four or five hundred years.*

* The version of early Roman constitutional history in this paragraph is corrected in L185, A10–D1: "Thus the sovereignty of the commonwealth lay in the body of the aristocrats and nobles, since by far the largest part of the people was assigned to the sixth class, which was that of the poorest and the lowest. Indeed, the rest of the classes together contained barely a tenth of the citizens. Since this was the place of the commons in the assembly and since its opinion was never taken, it began to cause disturbances. The result was three secessions to the Aventine hill, to which the commons withdrew in arms in order to defend its liberty and power against the aristocrats. It could not be mollified until it was allowed to create sacrosanct magistrates of its own, and to do so in the assembly by tribes (*tributis comitiis*) from which the patricians were excluded. The commoners, therefore, were quieted for a time by an arrangement in which the greater magistrates – the consuls, I say, the praetors, and the censors – were chosen in the assembly by centuries, that is, by the aristocrats; while the lesser magistrates were chosen in the assembly by tribes, that is, by the commons. Under that arrangement, the state appears to have been in some sense mixed. But anyone who tried to understand this very brief period and the disturbances therein, which shook the foundations of the commonwealth, would readily admit that the commonwealth was barely able to endure twenty or thirty years of that regime, and then only in extreme wretchedness, and could not have stayed in it even that long were it not hemmed in by enemies on every side. Indeed the commons, shortly after, got hold of the power to make law, in which the sovereignty of the commonweath resides, and little by little they wrested control of the remaining rights of sovereignty from a reluctant and stubbornly resistant aristocracy. Yet even in the time when the people (*populus*) chose the greater magistrates in the assembly by centuries, the commons (*plebs*) was there in the assembly and was counted in the sixth class; and even though it voted only very rarely, it could do so if the previous classes were divided – which suffices to show that even at that time the state was democratic."

Someone could still object that even if the forms of state cannot be mixed, it does not follow that there are only three. For it can happen that, of sixty thousand citizens, forty thousand have a share in sovereignty, and twenty thousand are excluded. Conversely, it can also happen that of sixty thousand, one or two hundred hold the sovereignty, or even twenty-nine thousand, which is still the lesser part of the people. Yet there is a considerable difference between a hundred men having power, and twenty-nine thousand; and between forty thousand and sixty thousand. My answer is that the degree of more or less is not to be considered so long as it is more or less than half. For if degree were used to determine the variety of states, there would be a million of them, or rather the number would be infinite since the increasing or decreasing number of those having a share in the state would entail an infinite diversity. And the infinite should always be excluded from any science or discipline.

Other objections that may be prompted by the specific nature of each form of state will be cleared up below. With respect to the present question, however, there is still one more objection that might be raised: namely, that the Roman state, when Augustus was emperor and for a long time afterwards,* was called a principate, which is a form of state that is never mentioned in Herodotus, Plato, **[269]**
65} Aristotle, or even in Polybius, who counted seven forms. We read in Suetonius that the emperor Caligula, seeing several kings whom he had invited to dinner getting into a debate on the honor and antiquity of their houses, loudly repeated the verse from Homer that Agamemnon spoke against Achilles when the latter sought to present himself as his peer and equal. " 'Let there be but one king,' Caligula said. And he was not far," says Suetonius, "from taking the crown and changing the form of the Roman principate into a kingship."†

But a principate is nothing other than a democracy or aristocracy in which there is a chief who can give commands to every individual, and

(In the Latin, it may be noted, Bodin acknowledges that the initial concessions to the commoners created a mixed constitution which, however, did not work. He also begins his remarks on this period by calling the earliest republican constitution an aristocracy, only to end by calling it democratic as in the French.)

*L186, A10 specifies, "up to Flavius Vespasian." IP, p. 564, n.47 calls this an explicit allusion to the *lex regia* which purported to transfer complete power to the emperor from the people, and is traditionally dated from Vespasian's reign.

†L186, B6–8 adds, "From this it is clear that under Augustus after the battle of Actium the state was neither a democracy, nor an aristocracy, nor yet a kingship."

is no more than first collectively (*et n'est que premier en nom collectif*). For the word *princeps*, taken strictly, merely means the first.* Thus the people of Judea† complained that Aristobulus, the first prince of the house of the Asmoneans, changed the principate, which was aristocratic, into a dyarchy (*double royaume*),‡ by taking one crown for himself and sending another to his brother. We find the same arrangement in the ancient towns of Tuscany, which entered into an alliance with Tarquinus Priscus, king of the Romans, on the condition that he would not have the power of life and death over them, and that he could not place garrisons in the towns, or levy taxes, or change anything in their customs and laws. *Sed ut civitatum principatus penes*
{566} *regem Romanum esset*,§ as Florus puts it. It is thus evident that the king of the Romans had no power over the towns of Tuscany except as he presided in their Estates (*sinon qu'il estoit le premier aux estats*). My answer to this last objection, then, is that in many aristocratic and democratic commonwealths there is one magistrate who is first among all in honor and authority – like the emperor in Germany, the duke in Venice, and the archon in ancient Athens – but that this does not change the form of state.¶

But the Roman emperors called themselves mere magistrates, commanders-in-chief, tribunes, and first citizens, even though in practice many behaved like monarchs and most of them were cruel tyrants. Moreover, they had the arms and the fortresses in their power, and in matters of state the master of brute force is the master of men, of the laws, and of the entire commonwealth.|| From a legal

*L186, B8–10 expands this, "But a principate is nothing but an aristocratic or democratic state in which one individual presides, and whom the Latins call *praetor* from *praeundo*, going in front, and *princeps*, that is, *primus*, first." (This effort to connect principate with praetor seems to have been a passing foray. It is not followed up.)

†L186, B10 has "the Jews."

‡For "dyarchy (*double royaume*)" L186, B11 substitutes, "two kingdoms (*duo regna*)."

§"But the power of the Roman king was to be that of a *princeps* in their commonwealths."

¶L186, D1–3 adds, "If there are two magistrates who share the same power, as at Rome; or three, as in many Swiss commonwealths; or four, as at Geneva, it cannot be called a principate because no one is the first."

||The point of this return to the Roman example is to show that it was a pseudo-principate. This is made clear in the Latin along with expanded comments at 186, D3–187, A1: "But in the Roman commonwealth, Augustus, shrewdly disguising his power, had himself named emperor – that is, supreme general of the army – as well as tribune of the people charged with protecting the people whom he had robbed of its liberty, and took a ten-year protectorship of the commonwealth that appeared to be all but forced upon him by the Senate. He thus established a principate by subterfuge and pretense. And since he had stationed forty legions throughout the provinces, kept three on hand as

standpoint, says Papinian, we must look not **[270]** to what they do at Rome, but to what they ought to do. It thus appears that a principate (*principauté*) is nothing other than an aristocracy or a democracy having some one person as president or leader (*premier*) who is yet bound by those who have the sovereignty.

a bodyguard, and secured the citadels and fortresses with garrisons, he in effect took royal power without scepter, diadem, or crown. His successors ruled tyrannically, with few exceptions each one more cruelly than the one before. At the beginning of his reign, says Suetonius, Tiberius rose in the presence of the consuls and made way for them, but at the end he inflicted the vilest of servitudes upon the commonwealth."

[297] BOOK II, CHAPTER 5

Whether it is lawful to make an attempt upon the tyrant's life and to nullify and repeal his ordinances after he is dead

Ignorance of the exact meaning of the term "tyrant" has led many people astray, and has been the cause of many inconveniences. We have said that a tyrant is someone who makes himself into a sovereign prince by his own authority – without election, or right of succession, or lot, or a just war, **[298]** or a special calling from God. This is what is understood by tyrant in the writings of the ancients and in the laws that would have him put to death. Indeed, the ancients established great prizes and rewards for those who killed tyrants, offering titles of nobility, prowess, and chivalry to them along with statues and honorific titles, and even all the tyrant's goods, because they were taken as true liberators of the fatherland, or of the motherland, as the Cretans say. In this they did not distinguish between a good and virtuous prince and a bad and wicked one, for no one has the right to seize the sovereignty and make himself the master of those who had been his companions, no matter what pretenses of justice and virtue he may offer. In strictest law, furthermore, {unauthorized} use of the pre-
{606} rogatives reserved to sovereignty is punishable by death. Hence if a subject seeks, by whatever means, to invade the state and steal it from his king or, in a democracy or aristocracy, to turn himself from a fellow-citizen into lord and master, he deserves to be put to death.* In this respect our question does not pose any difficulty.

It is true that the Greeks differed from the Latins as to whether, in this case, one should preempt resort to law by resort to force. The Valerian law, published at the request of P. Valerius Publicola,

*For "deserves to be put to death" L207, B7–8 substitutes, more forcefully, "may be killed by the people collectively or by any individual (*ab universis, et singulis occidi licere*)."

approved the latter, provided it was established afterwards that the person killed had indeed aspired to sovereignty. This seems to be a good solution. If judicial proceedings were required, the fire would be likely to have consumed the commonwealth before one could come to its rescue. How bring someone to trial who has armed guards around him and has seized the fortresses? Would it not be better to proceed by way of force rather than, in wishing to preserve the way of law, to lose the laws together with the state? Nevertheless, Solon passed a law to the opposite effect, which expressly forbade using force, or killing someone who was trying to seize sovereignty, until a trial was held and a verdict rendered. This seems more equitable than the Valerian law because there have been many good citizens and respectable people who have been killed by their enemies on the pretext that they aimed at tyranny; it was then easy to make a case against the dead.

But to harmonize these two laws, and to resolve the question, it seems to me **[299]** that Solon's law should apply when the individual suspected of tyranny has not yet collected forces or occupied strongpoints, and the Valerian law when the tyrant has openly declared himself or when he has seized control of citadels and garrisons. In the first situation, we find that the dictator Camillus proceeded judicially
7} against M. Manlius Torquatus; in the second, Brutus and Cassius killed Caesar. But Solon, for having been too scrupulous on this point, could not stop Pisistratus from turning himself from a subject and citizen into a master before his very eyes. And those who killed the tyrants of Athens did not proceed judicially.*

At this point there are many questions one may ask, such as whether a tyrant, who I said may be justly killed without form or shape of trial, becomes legitimate if, after having encroached upon sovereignty by force or fraud, he has himself elected by the Estates. For it seems that the solemn act of election is an authentic ratification of the tyranny, an indication that the people have found it to their liking. But I say that it is nevertheless permissible to kill him, and to do so by force unless the tyrant, stripping off his authority, has given up his arms and put power back into the hands of the people in order to have its judgment. What tyrants force upon a people stripped of power cannot be called consent. Sulla, for example, had himself made

*"And those who killed . . . judicially." Substitution at L207, D12–L208, A1 clarifies the reference and supplies details: "Harmodius and Aristogoton killed the sons of Pisistratus without regard to the law and on Solon's personal authority."

dictator for eighty years by the Valerian law, which he got published with a powerful army camped inside the city of Rome. But Cicero said that this was not a law. Another example is Caesar, who had himself made permanent dictator by the Servian law; and yet another is Cosimo de Medici who, having an army inside Florence, had himself
{608} elected duke. When objections were raised, he set off a volley of gunfire in front of the palace, which induced the lords and magistrates to get on with it more quickly.

But if a tyrant's successors have held sovereignty for a long period of time, such as a hundred years, then, here as in all other matters, the prescription of so long a period can serve as a title. Although it is said that sovereignty cannot be prescribed, that means in less than a hundred years, especially if there has been neither opposition nor protest by subjects to the contrary.* An example of the latter is the opposition of the tribune Aquila, who was brave enough to remove the crown that had been placed on Caesar's statue, **[300]** despite all the power that Caesar had, an act which so nettled Caesar that he added "If it please Aquila the Tribune" to all the orders and pardons that he issued.

So much then for the tyrant, whether virtuous or wicked, who makes himself a sovereign lord on his own authority. But the chief difficulty arising from our question [in this chapter] is whether a sovereign prince who has come into possession of the state by way of election, or lot, or right of succession, or just war, or by a special calling from God, can be killed if he is cruel, oppressive, or excess-

*For "But if a tyrant's successors . . . to the contrary" L208, B5–C10 substitutes an important clarification of what Bodin means by the imprescriptibility of sovereignty: "But if the tyrant's children and relations hold on to the tyranny transmitted by their forebears for a very long stretch of time, say one hundred years in unbroken succession, and govern the commonwealth with justice, then that regime should not be called a tyranny since the prescription of long time has legitimating force. What we have said about the rights of sovereignty not being prescriptible applies to private individuals who attempt to usurp the rights of sovereignty while the state (*respublica*) still stands, and not to an entire alteration of the state (*reipublicae*). We have specified 'without break or interruption,' which means that the citizens shall not have disturbed the ruler's possession by any conspiracy against the tyrant or his offspring, or by any opposition, since it is fairly evident from this that the citizens have truly acquiesced in his commands and have accepted him as a legitimate prince."

(The idea here is that specific prerogatives of sovereignty cannot be prescribed so long as the legitimate sovereign remains in being and is prepared to assert his right to sovereignty as a whole. But sovereignty as a whole can be transferred, and where sovereignty as a whole has been usurped rather than transferred voluntarily, the rule of prescription determines when it has become legitimate.)

ively wicked. For that is the meaning [ordinarily] given to the word tyrant.[1] Many doctors [of law] and theologians, who have touched upon this question, have resolved that it is permissible to kill a tyrant without distinction [as to the type],[2] and some, putting two words together that are incompatible, have spoken of a king-tyrant (*roi tyran*),[3] which has caused the ruin of some very fine and flourishing monarchies.

But to decide this question properly we need to distinguish between a prince who is absolutely sovereign and one who is not, and between subjects and foreigners. It makes a great difference whether we say that a tyrant can be lawfully killed by a foreign prince or by a subject. For just as it is glorious and becoming, when the gates of justice have been shut, for someone, whoever he may be, to use force in defense of the goods, honor, and life of those who have been unjustly oppressed – as Moses did when he saw his brother being beaten and mistreated and had no way of getting justice – so is it a most beautiful and magnificent thing for a prince to take up arms in order to avenge an entire people unjustly oppressed by a tyrant's cruelty, as did Hercules, who traveled all over the world exterminating tyrant-monsters and was deified for his great feats. The same was done by Dion, Timoleon, Aratus, and other generous princes, who obtained the title of chastisers and correctors of tyrants. This, furthermore, was the sole cause for which Tamerlane, prince of the Tartars, declared war on Bajazet [Bayazid I], who was then besieging Constantinople, Tamerlane saying that he had come to punish him for tyranny and to deliver the afflicted peoples. He defeated Bajazet in a battle fought on the plateau of Mount Stella, and after he had killed and routed three hundred thousand Turks, he had the tyrant chained inside a cage until he died. In this case it makes no **[301]** difference whether this virtuous prince proceeds against a tyrant by force, deception, or judicial means. It is however true that if a virtuous prince has seized a tyrant, he will obtain more honor by putting him on trial and punishing him as a murderer, parricide, and thief, rather than acting against him by the common law of peoples (*droit des gens*).*

*L209, B9–11 adds, "Let us then agree on this, that any foreigner is allowed to kill a tyrant, that is to say, someone whose infamy is on everybody's lips, and who is notorious for rapine, murders, and cruelties toward his subjects." (The Latin here, seemingly more permissive than the French, gives permission to any foreigner rather than to princes only. The difference is perhaps inadvertent since L213, B2–4, as in French 307 (p. 120 below), Bodin mentions only foreign princes.)

But as for subjects, and what they may do, one has to know whether the prince is absolutely sovereign, or is properly speaking not a sovereign. For if he is not absolutely sovereign, it follows necessarily that sovereignty is in the people or the aristocracy. In this latter case there is no doubt that it is permissible to proceed against the tyrant either by way of law if one can prevail against him, or else by way of fact and open force, if one cannot otherwise have justice. Thus the Senate took the first way against Nero, the second against Maximinus* [and legitimately so] inasmuch as the Roman emperors were no more than princes of the republic, in the sense of first persons and chief citizens, with sovereignty remaining in the people and the Senate.[4]

That state, as I have shown above, was called a principate even though Seneca, speaking in the person of his student, Nero, has him say, "I alone of all the living have been elected and chosen as God's
{*611*} lieutenant on earth. I am the arbiter of life and death; I am all-powerful and can dispose of every one's status and condition as I please." Nero, it is true, had in fact usurped that power, yet in law the state was but a principate in which the people was sovereign. This is also the Venetian system, and the Venetians condemned their duke, Marin Faliero, to death, and put many others to death as well, without form or semblance of trial, since Venice is an aristocratic principate wherein the duke is no more than a first citizen, with sovereignty residing in the Estates of the Venetian gentlemen.† Similarly, the German Empire is also an aristocratic principate where the emperor is the first and chief person, but the power and majesty of the Empire belong to the Estates which deposed the emperor Adolph in 1296 and Wenceslas in 1400 by formal proceedings in law, since they had jurisdiction and power over them.

We may say the same of the Spartan state which was a pure aristocracy in which there were two kings who had no **[302]** sovereign power and were nothing more than captains. This is the reason why they were condemned to pay fines for their misdeeds, as was Agesilaus, or condemned to death, as were Agis and Pausanias. In our own time this has {often} been done to the kings of Denmark and

*For "Thus the Senate took the first way against Nero, the second against Maximinus" L209, C6–8 substitutes, "as we read was done against Nero and Maximinus, for both were condemned by the Senate to capital punishment although there was no regular trial."

†The Venetian example is omitted in the Latin.

Sweden also, of which some were exiled, some died in prison, and others are in prison still because the nobility contends that they are only princes and are not sovereign, as we have shown. Hence they are subject to the Estates, which possess the right of election. This also applies to the ancient kings of Gaul, whom Caesar called *regulos*, or
2} petty kings, since they were subject to the authority and judicial power of the aristocrats who held the entirety of sovereignty and had them sentenced to death if they deserved it. This is why Ambiorix, the captain-in-chief, whom they called king of the *Liegeois*, said, "Our commands are such that the people has no less power over me than I over the people." He thus clearly indicates that he was not sovereign, although it is impossible that his power should have been equal to the people's, as we have demonstrated in our chapter on sovereignty.

But if the prince is sovereign absolutely, as are the genuine monarchs of France, Spain, England, Scotland, Ethiopia, Turkey, Persia, and Moscovy – whose power has never been called into question and whose sovereignty has never been shared with subjects – then it is not the part of any subject individually, or all of them in general, to make an attempt on the honor or the life of the monarch, either by way of force or by way of law, even if he has committed all the misdeeds, impieties, and cruelties that one could mention. As to the way of law, the subject has no right of jurisdiction over his prince, on whom all power and authority to command depends; he not only can revoke all the power of his magistrates, but in his presence, all the power and jurisdiction of all magistrates, guilds and corporations, Estates and communities, cease, as we have said and will say again even more elaborately in the proper place. And if it is not permissible for a subject to pass judgment on his prince, or a vassal on his lord, or a servant on his master – in short, if it [303] is not permissible to proceed against one's king by way of law – how could it be licit to do so by way of force? For the question here is not to discover who is the strongest, but only whether it is permissible in law, and whether a subject has the power to condemn his sovereign prince.

3} A subject is guilty of treason in the first degree not only for having killed a sovereign prince, but also for attempting it, advising it, wishing it, or even thinking it. And the law finds this so monstrous [as to subject it to a special rule of sentencing]. Ordinarily, if someone who is accused, seized, and convicted dies before he has been sentenced, his personal status is not diminished, no matter what his crime, even if

it was treason [in lesser form].* But treason in the highest degree can never be purged by the death of the person accused of it, and even someone who was never accused is considered in law as having been already sentenced.[5] And although evil thoughts are not subject to punishment, anyone who has thought of making an attempt on the life of his sovereign prince is held to be guilty of a capital crime, no matter whether he repented of it. In fact there was a gentleman from Normandy who confessed to a Franciscan friar that he had wanted to kill King Francis I but had repented of this evil wish. The Franciscan gave him absolution, but still told the king about it; he had the gentleman sent before the Parlement of Paris to stand trial, where he was condemned to death by its verdict and thereupon executed. And one cannot say that the court acted from fear [of the king], in view of
{614} the fact that it often refused to verify edicts and letters patent even when the king commanded it. And in Paris a man, named Caboche, who was completely mad and out of his senses, drew a sword against King Henry II without any effect or even attempt. He too was condemned to die without consideration of his insanity, which the law ordinarily excuses no matter what murder or crime the madman may have committed.

Lest one say that these laws and these verdicts have been made and handed down by men, we read in Holy Scripture that Nebuchadnezzar, king of Assyria, devastated the countryside of Palestine; besieged, entered, and pillaged the city of Jerusalem; razed houses and walls; burned down the Temple and desecrated God's sanctuary; killed the king and most of the people, **[304]** taking the rest to Babylon as slaves; set up a statue of gold there bearing his image and commanding everyone without exception to worship it on pain of being burned alive, and had those who refused to worship it thrown into a fiery furnace; yet for all of this the prophet [Jeremiah], in a letter to the Jews who were in Babylon, wrote that they should pray to God to give a good and happy life to Nebuchadnezzar and his children and to allow them to reign for as long as the skies should last.
{615} Was there ever a tyrant more detestable than this man who, not content with being worshipped in his person, ordered his likeness to be worshipped also on pain of being burned alive? Yet we see the prophet Ezekiel full of anger against Zedekiah, king of Jerusalem,

*L210, C10–11 is more specific; "unless he violated the safety or dignity of the prince."

heaping scorn upon him for his treachery, disloyalty, and rebellion against his king, Nebuchadnezzar, and asserting that he deserved nothing less than death.

We have an even more outstanding example in Saul, who was driven by an evil spirit to kill all the priests of God for no reason whatsoever, and made every effort to kill David or to have him killed. Yet David, who twice had Saul in his power, said, "God forbid that I should do violence to him whom God has consecrated," and prevented anyone from harming him in any way. When Saul was killed in war, and a soldier brought his head to David, he had the soldier put to death, saying, "Scoundrel! Dared you lay your impure hands on him whom God has consecrated? You shall die for that." This incident is especially noteworthy in that David had been unjustly marked for death by Saul and did not lack for power, as his enemies had reason to know. Moreover, he had been chosen by God to be king over the people and had been anointed by Samuel, and he had married the king's daughter. Yet even so he shrank from assuming royal status and, even more, from doing violence to the life of Saul or to his honor, or from rebelling against him, but preferred to leave the kingdom and go into voluntary exile.

6} We read also that the holiest individuals there ever were among the Hebrews, who were called the Essenes (meaning those who truly follow the law of God), held that sovereign princes, no matter **[305]** who they might be, ought to be inviolable to their subjects as having been anointed and sent by God. Nor can there be any doubt that David, who was both a king and a prophet and who had God's spirit if ever anybody had it, always kept before his eyes the command of God that says, "Thou shalt not speak ill of thy prince, and shalt not belittle the magistrates." There is nothing more frequent in Holy Scripture than the prohibition against killing or making any attempt on the life or honor not only of the king, but also of the magistrates, even if (says Scripture) they are wicked. If, therefore, an individual is guilty of violating divine and human majesty (*lèse maiesté divine et humaine*) merely for speaking ill of magistrates, what punishment can suffice for someone who makes an attempt upon their lives? For the law of God is even stricter in this matter than human law. Thus the *lex Julia* makes it treason to advise the killing of a magistrate or a commissioner entrusted with the power to command; but the law of God forbids any insult whatsoever to the magistrate.

{617} Replying to the frivolous objections and arguments of those who hold the contrary would be a waste of time. Just as someone who doubts the existence of God deserves to be punished according to the law without using arguments, so also do those who have cast doubt on a thing as clear as this, and have even published books which hold that subjects may justly take up arms against a tyrannical prince and put him to death by any means whatever. For even their own most prominent and learned theologians hold that it is never permissible to kill or even to rebel against one's sovereign prince unless by a special and unquestionable mandate from God, as in the example of Jehu, who was chosen by God and anointed king by the prophet [Elisha] with an express command to exterminate the house of Ahab.* Jehu was a subject, and despite all the cruelties, acts of extortion, and murders of prophets that King Ahab and Jezebel had committed, he made no attempt against his prince until he had an express command from God speaking through the mouth of the prophet. God in fact so favored him that, with but a small company, he put to death two kings, seventy children of Ahab, many other princes of the kings of Israel and Judea, and all the idol-worshipping priests, after having **[306]** fed the body of Queen Jezebel to the dogs. But one must not extend this special mandate of God to conspiracies and rebellions of mutinous subjects against a sovereign prince.

As for Calvin's remark that if there existed in these times magistrates especially constituted for the defense of the people and to restrain the licentiousness of kings, like the ephors in Sparta, the tribunes in Rome, and the demarchs in Athens, then those magistrates should resist, oppose, and prevent their licentiousness and cruelty† – it clearly shows that it is never licit, in a proper monarchy, to attack a sovereign king, or defend one's self against him, or to make an attempt upon his life or honor, for he spoke only of democratic and aristocratic states. I have shown above that the kings

* Bodin's note refers to Luther generally and to Calvin, *Commentary on the Epistle of John* and *Institutes of the Christian Religion* [to the chapter given as IV, 20, 31 in the last Latin edition of 1559].

† A loose translation of *Institutes*, IV, 20, 31. Omitted in Bodin's translation is the clause in which Calvin, speaking of ephors, tribunes, and demarchs, adds, "and perhaps even the power now possessed by the Three Estates of the several kingdoms when they meet in their assemblies." But Bodin clearly refers to that clause when, two sentences later, he archly notes that Calvin, speaking of the Estates, says, "possible, not daring to be definite."

of Sparta were but simple senators and captains. And when he [Calvin] speaks of the Estates [of our own time], he says "possible," not daring to be definite. In any event there is an important difference between attacking the honor of one's prince and resisting his tyranny, between killing one's king and opposing his cruelty.*

We thus read that the Protestant princes of Germany, before taking up arms against the emperor, asked Martin Luther if it were permissible. He frankly replied that it was not permissible no matter how great the charge of impiety or tyranny. But he was not heeded; and the outcome of the affair was miserable, bringing with it the ruin of some great and illustrious houses of Germany. *Quia nulla iusta causa videri potest*, said Cicero, *adversus patriam arma capiendi.*† Admittedly, it is quite certain that the sovereignty of the German Empire does not lie in the person of the emperor, as we shall explain in due course. But since he is the chief [person of the state], they could have taken up arms against him only with the consent of the Estates or its majority,
9} which was not obtained.‡ It would have been even less permissible against a sovereign prince.§

I can give no better parallel than that of a son with respect to his father. The law of God says that he who speaks evil of his father or his

*This entire paragraph is omitted at L212, C4. Calvin's doctrine of resistance is now acknowledged only in a marginal note and in a much softened and restrictive paraphrase, "[According to] Sleidan, in his *History* [*of the Reformation*], Calvin writes that the ephors could punish the kings as though they were private persons, but that no one else could" L212, n. 2.

This softening in the Latin may hark back to Bodin's position in the first edition which contains no reference to *Institutes* IV, 20, 31 either in the text or in the marginalia. IP 618, n. 39 notes that the textual material was added to the French with the edition of 1578.

† "Because there can never be just cause to take up arms against one's country."

‡ Bodin is assuming that armed resistance, even where legitimate, must always be authorized by a constituted authority like the ephors or the Estates. This was the standard view among constitutionalist theorists as well. See Franklin, *Constitutionalism and Resistance*.

§ "Admittedly, it is quite certain . . . sovereign prince" is in some respects more pointed in L212, C10–D6: "If the emperor Charles [V] had indeed subjected the citizens and the commonwealth to tyranny, he could have been lawfully killed because, as we have shown above, he did not possess the rights of sovereignty. But Luther did not point that out, and I do not know whether he was aware of that distinction. Nor did he consider that Charles and all the princes, with very few exceptions, were of one opinion with [that is, had the support of] the general community (*respublica*). He answered as if Charles alone had supreme authority, on which account it is much less lawful to take up arms against a king." The Latin, however, is less clear than the French on the need for the consent of the Estates in the German Empire as actually constituted.

mother shall be put to death. If the father be a murderer, a thief, a traitor to his country, a person who has committed incest or parricide, a blasphemer, an atheist, and anything else one wants to add, I confess that the entire gamut of penalties will not suffice for his punishment; but I say that it is not for his son to lay hands on him, *quia nulla tanta impietas, nullum tantum factum est quod sit parricidio vindicandum*,* as it was put by an **[307]** orator of ancient times. And yet Cicero, taking up this question, says that love of country is even greater {than love of parents}. Hence the prince of our country, being ordained and sent by God, is always more sacred and ought to be more inviolable than a father.

I conclude then that it is never permissible for a subject to attempt anything against a sovereign prince, no matter how wicked and cruel a tyrant he may be. It is certainly permissible not to obey him in anything that is against the law of God or nature – to flee, to hide, to evade his blows, to suffer death rather than make any attempt upon his life or honor. For oh, how many tyrants there would be if it were lawful to kill them! He who taxes too heavily would be a tyrant, as the vulgar understand it; he who gives commands that the people do not like would be a tyrant, as Aristotle defined a tyrant in the *Politics*; he who maintains guards for his security would be a tyrant; he who
{*620*} punishes conspirators against his rule would be a tyrant. How then should good princes be secure in their lives? I would not say that it is illicit for other princes to proceed against tyrants by force of arms, as I have stated, but it is not for subjects.

Even so my preferred view is that of Diogenes the Cynic. One day, having met Dionysius the Younger in Corinth, where he had been exiled for his tyranny, and having watched him enjoy himself in the streets with jesters and musicians, chatting with them about their acts, Diogenes, putting on his best manner, said to him, "You are now in a condition unworthy of you." "I am grateful to you for your sympathy," said Dionysius. "Do you think," said Diogenes, "that I said that from compassion? It was rather because I saw a slave like you, who should have grown old and died as did your father in the unhappy condition of a tyrant, enjoying himself in safety and having a pleasant time among us, despite the life that you have led." Could one have more cruel executioners than fear and terror? I am speaking of the

* "Because there is no impiety so great, and no crime so great that it ought to be avenged by parricide."

perpetual fear and terror of losing one's life, one's possessions, one's state, and all of one's relatives and friends. This is the way it always is for tyrants, who constantly tremble for their lives and harbor a thousand suspicions, envies, rumors, jealousies, desires for revenge, and other passions that tyrannize the tyrant more cruelly than he could tyrannize his slaves with all the torments he might imagine. What greater misfortune **[308]** could befall a man than that which drives and forces the tyrant to make his subjects brutish and stupid, to cut them off from all the paths of virtue and honest learning, to subject them to a thousand spies and agents in order to know what they are doing, what they are saying, and what they are thinking, and, instead of joining and uniting his subjects in true friendship, sowing a hundred thousand quarrels and dissensions among them so that they may always be distrustful of each other? Who would doubt that a tyrant dwelling amid such evils is not more afflicted and tormented than if he had died a thousand times? Theophrastus said that death is the end of one's miseries, and Caesar said that it is the peace of the unhappy (both of them speaking as if there were no punishment set for the wicked after this life is done). Therefore, to want the tyrant killed so that he may suffer the [earthly] penalty he deserves is to seek his peace and well-being.

Nevertheless, the majority of tyrants ordinarily have favorites and parasites around them whom they can blame so that the people, roused to fury, discharge it upon them. Tiberius thus had Seianus; Nero, Tigellinus; Dionysius the Younger, Philistus; and Henry, king of Sweden, George Preschon [Pehrsson] – all of whom were made victims of people's fury. And did not the emperor Caracalla, to obtain the favor of the people, have all the sycophants killed whom he had induced to kill his brother? Caligula did the same to the sycophants around him. By such means tyrants have often managed to escape.

But if revenge began with the person of the tyrant, his agents and his closest relatives were also killed, including his wife and daughters. This was done not only everywhere in Greece but in Sicily too where, after the death of the tyrant Hieronymus, his sisters and cousins were cruelly dismembered by the people in its rage. Beyond that, all the domestic servants of the tyrant are ordinarily killed and his statues smashed. And often all his edicts are repealed, even if they were commendable and necessary, so that no vestige of the tyrant may remain, although quite often good ordinances of the tyrant are

{622} retained. That is why Cicero said that there was nothing more vulgar than to approve a tyrant's acts while praising to the skies those who killed him. But in another place he says that the question of **[309]** whether an upright man should attend the council of a tyrant for something that is good and advantageous to the public, is a difficulty that has not been resolved.

Nevertheless, this latter question depends upon the one preceding. If one refuses on grounds of conscience to attend the tyrant's council even for a good purpose for fear of giving approval to his tyranny, how then approve the good laws and ordinances he may have made? For this too ratifies the tyranny, and commends its example, no less than counseling the tyrant to do good and commendable things. On the other hand, one might want to say that a tyranny, when it is strong and functioning, gains support and authority when it secures the counsel of decent men for some good and commendable act, while a tyrant once dead is not resuscitated by the ratification of his acts, which often have to be retained out of sheer necessity if one is not to ruin the commonwealth completely.* Thus the captain Thrasibulus, after driving out the thirty tyrants at Athens, and Aratus, after defeating the tyrant of Syracuse, and, following their example, Cicero, after the death of the dictator Caesar, published laws of oblivion designed to extinguish the appetite for vengeance and ratifying, for the most part, acts of the tyrants that could not be suppressed without completely ruining the commonwealth. And when we read that the acts, edicts, and ordinances of Nero and Domitian were suppressed by the
{623} Senate, this applies only to their bad and unjust acts.† Were it otherwise, the ruin of the Empire would soon have followed, for during the first five years that he was emperor, Nero's laws and ordinances were excellent and his acts commendable, which led Trajan to conclude that Nero had no equal [in that respect].

This is why the jurists and doctors of law have held that the successor of a tyrant is bound by the tyrant's legitimate acts and

*For "which often . . . ruin the commonwealth completely" L214, C3–4 substitutes; "But not only should the advantageous measures of tyrants be ratified, but very often the iniquitous as well if we wish to save the commonwealth."

†"this applies only to their bad and unjust acts" is modified at L214, C9–D1, consistent with the thought (see note preceding) that at least some bad acts must be overlooked: "pertained [only] to certain standing edicts that would have introduced permanent injustice unless they were abrogated, and would have ruined what was now rightly ordered."

promises. Thus the emperor Constantine the Great, by an express edict, suppressed the acts of Licinius that were contrary to common law and ratified the rest. A similar decree was issued by the emperors Theodosius the Younger and Arcadius after the tyrant Maximus was defeated. *Quae tyrannus*, it reads, *contra ius rescripsit, non valere praecipimus, legitimis eius rescriptis minime impugnandis.** And although these two young emperors, in revenge against Maximus, passed a general edict by which **[310]** they cancelled all the benefices, positions, gifts, and offices he had conferred, and even annulled all the decisions and judgments rendered by him, still, in issuing their edict,
24} they ratified and confirmed all acts and commissions that had been obtained without deceit and fraud.

These words "without deceit and fraud" are put in to foil the sycophants, agents, and intermediaries of tyrants, to whom one should pay special attention, so that no one will follow their example of building one's own house on the ruin of another's during a time of tyranny, or when the commonwealth is divided by the disorders of a civil war. This is what happened at Milan when the Venetians, the French, the Swiss, the Spanish, and the Sforzas fought for power there. The jurist Jason [da Maino], among others, obtained, as a gift,† the possessions of M. Trivulce, who had sided with the house of France. But when the French came back, Trivulce defeated Jason by appealing to Jason's own legal commentaries and decisions. Nevertheless, a case like this hinges less on positive laws and precedents than on natural equity, which rests on the judgment of those who know how to handle affairs of state and to strike a sensible balance between individual advantage and the public good according to the diversity of times, places, and persons. The public good should always be given greater weight and preferred to a particular interest unless equity and reason are clearly against it. If, for example, tax collectors had been summoned and constrained to make payments to enemies or to a tyrant, that is good reason for allowing them credit for it, as was determined by a decision of the Parlement of Naples in a case involving persons who had made payments to the tax collectors of King Charles VIII. When, after the Spanish returned, there was some
25} thought of making the tax collectors pay twice, natural reason

*"We declare that unlawful decrees of the tyrant are invalid, but that his lawful decrees are not to be impugned."

†For "as a gift" L215, A8–9 substitutes, "by clever fraud."

prevailed over public advantage. But if tax collectors, acting without any summons or constraint, or perhaps pretending certain pressures on them, should take it upon themselves to make payments to a tyrant or to enemies, they could not only be justly constrained to pay all over again, but could also be found guilty of treason.*

To conclude this question, then, the good ordinances and worthy acts of a tyrant who has been killed should not be repealed. It is thus a great mistake on the part of princes [311] to repeal all the acts of tyrant-predecessors. But it is an even worse mistake to give rewards to those who killed a tyrant and thereby smoothed the successors' path to sovereignty. For the lives of the successors will never be secure unless they punish the assassins as Emperor Severus very wisely did in putting to death all of those who had a part in the murder of Emperor Pertinax. This, according to Herodian, was the reason why no one dared to make an attempt upon his life. The emperor Vitellius put to death all the assassins and conspirators against Galba who had presented Emperor Otho with signed requests for a reward for their disloyalty. And Theophilus, the emperor at Constantinople, summoned all of those who had made his father emperor after they had killed Leo the Armenian so that he could reward them for so great a deed. But when they came they were executed, along with many others who had not been involved.† Even more cruelly, the emperor Domitian had Epaphroditus, Nero's {freedman and} secretary of state, put to death for helping Nero commit suicide, even though Nero had insistently requested it.‡ Thus did David treat those who killed Saul and his son and thought they would have a great reward

† "If, for example, tax collectors . . . guilty of treason." The story is clarified at L215, B9–C6: "If, for example, the keepers of the treasury (*quaestores*) in the heat of a civil war, or during a time of tyranny, or during the invasion of fortresses and towns by a more lawful sort of enemy, are forced to pay out public funds, it ought to be credited as a payment for the commonwealth. Thus the high court of Naples decided in favor of the public debtors who paid what they owed to the tax collectors of King Charles VIII of France, and could not have done otherwise since the French were in control of the kingdom of Naples and determined its affairs. But if [public] debtors, acting without a prior summons or making an agreement with the enemy, should pay a part of what they owe in order to obtain a release from the rest, it is clear that they are not only liable for the entire sum but may be tried for treason."

† L215, D9–10 adds that these others had been "drawn there by the prospect of sharing in rewards."

‡ L215, A1–4 supplies a missing transition: "These things, we read, were done not only by tyrants but even by the best of kings, and not so much for their own safety as out of respect for those who had been killed."

for it. And Alexander the Great had Darius' murderer cruelly executed, horrified that any subject should have dared to lay hands
26} upon his king, even though he had been Alexander's enemy in a properly declared war.

Yet it seems to me that what has most kept the kings of France and their persons inviolable is that they have never inflicted cruel punishments on blood relatives even though they may have been seized, convicted, declared guilty, and condemned as enemies of their prince and guilty of treason. For example, John II, duke of Alençon, was condemned as a traitor in correct judicial form and a sentence of death was pronounced against him by the chancellor. Yet King Charles VII did not permit his execution. Many have criticized this leniency as pernicious. But they do not see that he who delivers a prince of the blood into the hands of the executioner, or has him assassinated, forges a weapon against himself. For we have seen ancient and modern emperors of Constantinople, as well as various kings of Spain and England, who chose to soil their hands with the blood of princes, [312] suffer in their own persons what they did to others. A single prince of the house of Castile killed six of his brothers, and in less than thirty-six years, eighty princes of the blood of England were cruelly murdered or killed at the hands of the executioner (as we read in Philip de Commines). Yet the greatest security for a prince is that he be regarded as sacred and inviolable.*

I know that Seleucus has been criticized for not having killed Demetrius the Besieger, one of the most valiant princes there ever was, when he held him prisoner; and Hugh Capet for having kept the
27} last prince of the line of Charlemagne in prison; and King Henry I of England for having kept his elder brother Robert in prison until he died; and Christierna, the father of King Frederick of Denmark, for having kept his cousin, the king of Denmark, in prison for twenty-five years until he died in the castle of Kalundborg at the age of seventy-five; and King John of Sweden who since 1567 has been holding his elder brother Henry prisoner; and the queen of England for maintaining her cousin as a prisoner, who had consistently claimed that the two kingdoms belong to her.† But by adopting this course these rulers

*L216, C5–8 adds, "It is also very important for the commonwealth that the royal stock be sacrosanct, for if all the princes were removed, the commonwealth might collapse or be torn asunder by interminable civil wars, as we shall show in due course."

†L217, A1–2 notes that, 'she [Elizabeth] seems to want to restore her [Mary's] rights and liberty in both kingdoms some day, and we hope it will be soon."

have had, and continue to have, more respect from their subjects than if they had put them to death.

I will be told that keeping such princes in prison is dangerous, and I admit it. Indeed, this was the main reason why the pope advised Charles of France to kill Conradin, the son of King Manfred of Naples, and why {Ptolemy} the last king of Egypt had Pompey killed, saying that dead men do not bite. Nevertheless, there were heirs
{628} enough of the house of Aragon to go on fighting the heirs of the house of Anjou, and to get back the kingdom. Meanwhile, the person who put Conradin to death was subsequently sentenced to die himself, and although he escaped, the infamy of a detestable cruelty committed without cause upon the person of an innocent young prince continued to lie on those who had him killed.[6] And when Duke John of Burgundy was pardoned for the murder of Duke Louis of Orleans, everyone said that from then on the blood of princes would be cheap. And so it turned out, for the same was done to John, and in cold blood.

Textual notes

Introduction

1 See Franklin, "Sovereignty and the Mixed Constitution."
2 Franklin, *Bodin and Absolutist Theory*, pp. 35ff.
3 *Ibid.*, pp. 23–25.
4 For a historical survey of the issue of *merum imperium* in medieval and post-medieval legal theory going back to the thirteenth century, see Myron P. Gilmore, *Argument from Roman Law* (Cambridge, Mass., 1941).
5 Alciato, *Paradoxa*, cols. 29ff.
6 *Methodus* (1951), pp. 174–76; *République* (1961), pp. 432ff.
7 *Juris universi distributio* (1951), p. 78.
8 Franklin, *Bodin and the Sixteenth-Century Revolution*, pp. 36ff.
9 *Ibid.*, pp. 37ff. See also Kelley, *Language, Law, and History.*
10 Franklin, *Bodin and the Sixteenth-Century Revolution*, pp. 59ff.
11 *Methodus*, pp. 174–75. In Book I, chapter 10 of the *République*, the list is expanded to include the right to receive oaths of fealty and homage, to determine the coinage and weights and measures, and taxation. For the most part these are elaborations of the basic five elements set down in the *Methodus.*
12 *Ibid.*, p. 177.
13 Locke, *Two Treatises*, II, 152 (pp. 368–69).
14 Seyssel, *Monarchy of France*, Part I, chapters 8–12 (pp. 49–58).
15 Franklin, *Bodin and Absolutist Theory*, pp. 34ff.
16 Cf. *ibid.*, pp. 38–40, and also Gierke, *The Development of Political Theory*, p. 161.
17 Bodin, *République* (1961), Preface.
18 For the main resistance doctrines of the time, see Franklin, *Constitutionalism and Resistance*. On the more general doctrinal and political setting for assertions of a right of resistance and revolution in the period, see Skinner, *Foundations*, II, 3.
19 Bodin, *République* (1961), Preface.
20 See Franklin, *Bodin and Absolutist Theory*, pp. 79ff.

21 *Ibid.*, pp. 70–79.
22 See Church, *Constitutional Thought*, chapter 3.
23 Bodin, *République* (1961), Epistola (dedicatory letter first added in the third edition, 1578).

Note on the text

1 McRae (ed.), *Six Bookes of a Commonweale*, p. A78.

Book I, chapter 8

1 Book I, chapter 9 in the first edition, but 1, 8 in all subsequent editions.
2 Bodin often uses the term "sovereign prince" or "prince" generically as the equivalent of sovereign.
3 In Bodin and most other authors of the period, the term "the law" or "written law," without any other qualifier, almost always refers to Roman civil law.
4 In Book III, chapter 2, Bodin defines an officer as a public person having an ordinary charge established by a standing law, whereas a commissioner is a public person given a temporary extraordinary charge.
5 Refers to one or both of the decemvirates, or magistracies held by ten men, appointed in 451 and 450 BC to draw up a code of laws for Rome.
6 Roman legislative acts were named for the magistrate or tribune who had brought the bill before an assembly of the people to request its passage. The bill or request was called a *rogatio*; if and when it was passed, it was called a *lex*.
7 Each of the tribunes of the people at Rome had a right of veto (*intercessio*) against the act of any magistrate (including even acts of a dictator in the classical republic), proceedings of the Senate, or elections and legislation by the assemblies.
8 A reference presumably to the *lex Antonia* of 44 BC, which was, however, passed only after Caesar's death.
9 Not all non-elective monarchies are technically hereditary. Some, like the French, may descend within the family by a public law, rather than by the private law of intestate inheritance or testamentary disposition.
10 The issue in this paragraph, which is not made very clear, is whether absolute power acquired by usurpation, and so without defined limit of time, is truly sovereign.
11 The law protects unjust possession against the use of force by private parties and thus allows the law to take its course.
12 Bodin is thus interpreting extension of power by tacit consent as a kind of precarious tenure.
13 Reigned 1574–89 as Henry III.
14 The *regalia* were privileges and prerogatives, mostly fiscal or ceremonial, belonging to the king by feudal law. The most celebrated list of *regalia* was the *Constitutio de regalibus* laid down in 1158 at the Diet of Roncaglia by the emperor Frederick I Barbarossa. Included in the *Libri Feudorum*, II, 56

(*Quae sint regalia*), which was attached to the *Corpus Juris* in the Middle Ages, it was often glossed by the civilians.

15 "Action of the law" {*legis actio*}, in Bodin's usage, is that part of a magistrate's jurisdiction requiring strict execution of the law without exercise of equitable discretion.

16 Bodin usually speaks of the law of God and the law of nature almost "in one breath," as Wimmer puts it (210, n. 98), even though he would not necessarily hold that the two are identical in content, that is, that the law of God contains nothing not given by natural reason.

17 As described here, observance by the ruler of the law of nature seems to be a condition of obedience, and at odds with Bodin's views on non-resistance (see below, p. 115). Even in a kingship passing by succession, that condition could be embodied in the fundamental law of succession and the oath of coronation, as in the Carinthian procedure discussed below. Bodin seems unaware of any difficulty, however, possibly because he lacks a concept of constituent power and cannot imagine any power remaining in the people authoritatively to take cognizance of a violation of the law of nature. For Bodin, that act of cognizance would imply retention of ordinary governmental power, which, *ex hypothesi*, has been entirely vested in the prince.

18 This last sentence seems intended merely to note that the duke of Carinthia was not a sovereign in international law, and not to modify the value of his coronation oath as an illustration of Bodin's principle.

19 The justice of Aragon was a medieval judge charged with defending the rights and privileges of the community.

20 This oath was widely cited by monarchomach constitutionalists and resistance theorists as an example of a coronation ceremony that expressed the right of the people *vis-à-vis* a tyrant-king. It was also connected with the idea of original election. For a critical history of the oath see Giesey, *If Not, Not: The Oath of the Aragonese and the Legendary Laws of Sobrarbe*.

21 Oldrado's holding in *Consilia*, 69, which Bodin cites, does not, however, bear on the power of the king of France *vis-à-vis* his own subjects, but affirms only that the king of France does not recognize the German emperor as a superior either *de jure* or *de facto*.

22 This last is the *ius gentium* which, translated as "the law of nations," suggests international law. But in Bodin's time and earlier, the primary meaning is the law (other than the laws of God and of nature) common to all peoples, or as Bodin puts it in the Latin, *lex omnium gentium communis*. At L84, D1–2 he speaks of "the law common to all peoples, the grounds (*rationes*) of which are different from the laws of nature and of God."

23 The Latin *lex* (law) is from *ligere* (to bind).

24 "Derogation" as Bodin explains (L85, B5–6) is partial repeal, as distinct from "abrogation," or complete repeal.

25 Since they would then be truly perpetual, as the Latin somewhat more clearly indicates (85, D1). This is because in a democracy or aristocracy the sovereign person never dies (and neither does the corporate body to

which the privilege is given). In any system, of course, a grant in perpetuity would appear to be revocable, given what Bodin says below about a sovereign not being bound by his own acts (p. 12). But the grant would not lapse *unless* revoked if given in perpetuity by a collective sovereign. A grant in perpetuity by a "natural" sovereign, or prince, on the other hand, would presumably become invalid on his death and would not be honored by the courts (see below, p. 18, n.*).

26 The sovereign courts were the high judicial and administrative tribunals considered to be direct extensions of the king. Of these the most important was the Parlement of Paris, which even claimed to be the Senate of the kingdom and to have important legislative powers.

27 Bodin's point is that oaths which simply invoke divine sanction for a promise do not bind if the promise does not bind.

28 A general derogation states that all legislation to the contrary is overridden, whereas a special derogation makes particular mention of the laws to be set aside, and thus puts more constraint upon the prince. A special derogation is required to change a law which the prince has sworn to keep, since he must be presumed not to will any change in it unless he has said so most expressly.

29 The main point of this paragraph seems to be that a law is never in itself a contract, even though it can be the subject of a contract or a promise.

30 An old unit of copper money having very low value. Note also that this entire discussion supposes that subsidies could not be lawfully imposed without consent.

31 The distinction here is between a promise to maintain all the laws as a condition of office, and the promise of a reigning king to maintain some specific law or laws as discussed in the preceding paragraph.

32 The oath reported by Bodin does not seem to fit very well with absolute authority. But his account, it may be noted, concerns only the designation of Henry V of England as the heir to the French throne. He did not in fact succeed to it.

33 Refers generally and vaguely to resistance treatises that began to appear among the French Protestants in the aftermath of the St. Bartholomew's Day Massacre of 1572. At the time of the first edition of Bodin's work in 1576, the best known of these was *Du droit des magistrats sur leurs subiets* by Théodore de Bèze, published anonymously at Geneva in 1574.

34 Since Bodin uses the term "democracy" only for the direct rule of the people's assembly, a representative government must, as here, be termed a kind of aristocracy. This usage was frequent at the time.

35 An apparent reference to his comment on the Epirote oath, on which see p. 16 above. This remark is retained at L90, D5–6, even though the Epirote oath has now been reinterpreted in an opposite sense.

36 On Bodin's view of taxation see Introduction, above.

37 A direct contradiction of Commines, who argued that there is always time. See *Mémoires*, V, 19.

38 Book V, chapter 2, pp. 877ff. (not translated).

39 Polydore Virgil (1470–1555), *Historiae Anglicae libri XXVII* is Bodin's main source for early English history.
40 The sense of *subside extraordinaire* in this context seems to be a new tax as distinguished from a customary revenue, rather than an emergency levy.
41 Henry VI had been set aside as king by Edward IV, who had himself proclaimed king in 1461 during the Wars of the Roses.
42 Verification here refers to the process of registering and incorporating royal decrees as authentic and legitimate expressions of the royal will. Bodin excludes any claims of a true right of veto associated with this function. The effect of verification by the Parlement or any other authoritative body, as he understands it, was to forestall further questions (and obstruction) by other magistrates.
43 Refers to one of the two great zones of law into which France was divided. The northern parts of France, roughly speaking, were the regions of customary law (*les pays de droit coutumier*), while the southern parts were the regions of written, or Roman, law (*les pays de droit écrit*). Roman law could be cited in the *pays de droit coutumier* where custom was defective; in the *pays de droit écrit* Roman law, as modified by usage, was itself the custom or common law.
44 The *lex regia* was the name used by the classical Roman jurists for the *lex de imperio* by which the Roman people was supposed to have conferred all of its power on the emperor at the beginning of each reign. Thus *Dig.*, I, 4, 1 (Ulpian) and *Cod.*, I, 17, 1, 7.
45 As distinct, therefore, from accession by election.
46 In his elaborate theory of the influence of climate and related factors on the character of peoples (*Methodus*, chapter 5; *République*, V, 1), Bodin holds that peoples of the north are resistant to strong authority and exhibit weakened forms of sovereignty. Peoples of the south, on the other hand, incline to extreme forms of authority, while peoples of the middle region (such as the French) are inclined to moderate and tempered forms of governance.
47 On the question of perjury arising from oaths to keep a law (primarily in self-governing cities) see Franklin, *Bodin and Absolutist Theory*, p. 60, n. 22, and p. 61, n. 24.
48 Note again the tendency to identify a mixed or limited monarchy with democracy. Cf. p. xviii, n.* above. But the point is softened at L94, C5–6.
49 A means of publicizing decrees at Athens.
50 The king in question was actually Ahasuerus.
51 The Twelve Tables was the earliest code of laws at Rome, drawn from customary law that was collected and codified by the Decemvirs in the middle of the fifth century BC. The original formulae survive only in fragments.
52 Peter Lombard (*c.*1100–*c.*1160). The *Sentences* is a compilation of theological opinions.
53 A law restricting the size of bequests that could be conferred on women.
54 *Retraict lignager* is the right of the relatives of a deceased to redeem an

inheritance that the deceased had alienated. The redemption had to take place within a certain period of time. The king is here represented as refusing to honor an assertion of such right of repurchase.

55 Bodin perhaps is a little unfair to Charles Du Moulin, whom he calls, nonetheless, "my colleague, the glory of all the jurists" (L101, B8). Du Moulin's position on the use of Roman law was much the same as Bodin's. See IP, p. 394, n. 97, and Franklin, *Bodin and the Sixteenth-Century Revolution*, p. 38.

56 The King Stephen mentioned by John of Salisbury, Bodin's source, was the king of England, not of Spain, and therefore issued his decree not for Spain but for England.

57 Against the practice, therefore, of going to Roman law where such gaps occurred.

58 The point throughout this discussion of the use of Roman law is that it is never binding by its own intrinsic authority, but only in so far as it has been incorporated either by deliberate act of the sovereign, or else by custom. Either way the sovereign is not bound by it except in so far as it embodies natural law. Neither of the French uses described in note 43 above would thus conflict with the ruler's sovereignty.

59 In this context, "taking" seems to mean the waiver, by the public, in order to make peace, of a private party's legitimate claim against a foreign state or individual.

60 A *lettre de restitution* released its recipient from an inequitable obligation.

61 Throughout this discussion it is implied that suits against the king are entertained by his consent, which is, however, presumed by the courts.

62 The conveyances to Rome attributed to Attalus and Eumenes were actually one conveyance by Attalus III of Pergamum.

63 For a brief summary of the civilian tradition as to the binding force of royal contracts on successors, see Franklin, *Bodin and Absolutist Theory*, pp. 80–84.

64 A king by testament is strictly bound because he holds of his predecessor and replaces him as would a private heir. A king by successive right who holds by public law, rather than by his predecessor's will, is not in the position of a private heir any more than is a king by election. Neither is bound directly by his predecessor's acts. Cf. L106, C2–7.

65 *Olim* (from the Latin for "formerly") is the short title of the collection of decrees and judgments of the Parlement of Paris 1254–1318. Of the seven original volumes, four remain.

Book I, chapter 10

1 This interpretation of I Samuel 10:25 by Melanchthon was also contested by the constitutionalists in the sixteenth century, and the controversy over this passage in Samuel became a conventional topic of debate among publicists of the period.

2 A loose rendition of *Politics*, Book IV, chapter 11, para. 1.

3 "modern (*les derniers*)" here refers to medieval commentators on Roman civil law. "Ancients (*les premiers*)" presumably refers to jurists of the Roman Empire, who did not, however, write on "regalian rights." Hence it is just possible that Bodin meant by "ancients" the *glossators*, or earlier medieval jurists.

4 When Bodin speaks of this right he almost always means the power of creating and defining the office as well as appointing the incumbent, although the term *eslire* (*eligere*), which he sometimes uses, might be taken as meaning "to appoint" only.

5 The thought here appears to be that these deputies cannot have obtained the status of sovereigns by prescription of long time so long as they continue to acknowledge dependency by the very nature of their titles. See L149, A10.

6 On the office of dictator at Rome see above, p. 3.

7 In Roman usage, the people as a whole (*populus* or *populus universus*) included the nobility and met in the *comitia centuriata*, so called because it was initially an assembly by military classes. The *comitia centuriata* was highly oligarchic in its allocation of voting power. When the acts of the *plebs*, or commoners, were accorded the status of laws, its assemblies became known as the *comitia tributa*, or assembly by tribes. Although voting rights here were more democratic, equality was gradually undermined by the maldistribution of population among the tribes into which the people were divided. Although the *comitia tributa* excluded the descendants of the original patriciate, it included the "new" nobility who were technically non-patrician by birth. Hence as time went on, the *comitia tributa* came pretty close to including the whole people in fact. Given this complexity, Bodin sometimes has trouble with terminology, *Menu peuple* (commoners) is too narrow in its connotation, while *peuple* is too broad in its denotation. It is not always clear, furthermore, whether *peuple* is being used for the *comitia tributa*, or the *comitia centuriata* since the latter, slightly reformed, still functioned in the later Republic.

8 Bodin appears to be inaccurate both as to the sequence and the details of these measures. The *Lex Valeria Horatia* is traditionally dated 449 BC, and, although it acknowledged acts of the *plebs* as laws, they were to become so only after approval by the Senate. Philo's measures date from 339 BC and, although confirming that plebiscites were laws, required that they be approved *in advance* by the Senate. The definitive constitutional breakthrough, therefore, was the *Lex Hortensia* of 287 BC, which gave plebiscites full status as laws without any need for approval by the Senate.

9 In accord with Roman legislative nomenclature, the term *Iuliae* in *leges Iuliae* refers to Augustus' gentile name (Julius). A *lex Iulia* means a law made at the request or proposal (*rogatio*) of Augustus Julius Caesar, and so avoids an explicit assertion of unilateral legislative power by the *Imperator*.

10 The term power (*potestas*, French *puissance*) rather than sovereignty (*maiestas*) is presumably used for the commons and the *comitia tributa* because the plebiscite, although held equivalent to law, was not exactly law; thus the Romans, with their well-known conservatism, could still

think of an act of the *comitia centuriata* as in some sense higher and more solemn.

11 Bodin evidently regards the entity that he calls the Council of Sages as an expanded version of the Council of Ten.

12 On the connection between the power to make law and the other prerogatives of sovereignty, see above, Introduction, p. xvi.

13 For Bodin's apparent confusion on the *lex Sulpicia* and *lex Martia*, see IP, p. 496, n. 44.

14 The war (90–88 BC) between Rome and her rebellious Italian allies (*socii*) which was finally settled by granting the Italians Roman citizenship.

15 Technically an inspector of pigs' tongues, perhaps to check for leprosy as noted by IP, p. 503, n. 65.

16 The point of this paragraph is that the right of magistrates, feudal or otherwise, to appoint subordinate officers is not a mark of sovereignty.

17 These were the basic territorial units of direct royal administration in the Old Regime, and are so peculiarly French that an attempt to translate them would be misleading as well as pointless. The *bailliage* and *seneschaussée* were loosely subordinate to the *gouvernement*, which was the largest regional administration.

18 The contradiction may not be immediately evident given all the qualifications Bodin includes in his response. But the point apparently is that, at least with Hadrian, the right of judgment in the last instance seems to have been vested in a subordinate authority.

19 Although *baillis* and *seneschaux* are French officers, the terms are here being used generically, and are applied to Germany as well as France.

20 The presidial courts were a network of tribunals, created in 1552, which were roughly intermediate between the *bailliages* and the Parlements.

21 *Requête civile* (*requeste civile*) was an extraordinary petition for reconsideration specifically designed for cases in which there was no right of appeal. The case was ordinarily reviewed by the judge against whose verdict the request was made, and that, apparently, is why it was called a "civil," or polite, request.

22 In the Old Regime, the term *président* was often used for the presiding judge of a judicial tribunal.

23 A grant made for the support of dependent members of the royal family.

24 Throughout this discussion of appeals, the term "sovereignty" is linked to the term "appeal" almost as a synonym, as though echoing an older usage in which the primary meaning of sovereignty was the right to hear appeals in last instance.

25 That is, so far as the effectiveness of royal power was concerned.

26 Exchequer was the name used for the high court of Normandy until it was turned into a Parlement in the course of the sixteenth century. The region of Alençon in Normandy had its own exchequer which was independent of the provincial high tribunal by virtue of the concession made to its dukes.

27 The letter of remission was accorded to someone who had committed homicide involuntarily or in self-defense, while the letter of pardon applied to non-capital offenses. The point here is that when such letters

were granted by the king, the latter could be reviewed by judges, the former could not.

28 A letter of justice, issued by the king, permitted the recipient to challenge a civil or criminal judgment. It was thus a mechanism for initiating an appeal.

29 Book I, chapter 9 (not translated here).

30 Refers to Bodin's monograph of 1568 on the causes of the price inflation of the sixteenth century. *La response de Jean Bodin a M. de Malestroit.*

31 The French terms *taille* and *impost* broadly refer to direct and indirect taxes respectively. But the usage is so loose that no consistent rule is adopted for the translation.

32 The four circumstances are: to pay for an overseas journey by the lord; for marrying his daughters; for his ransom if captured; for knighting his sons.

33 These were sovereign courts dealing respectively with fiscal oversight and with litigation arising from taxation.

34 In Bodin's *Methodus* (1566), the power to tax is not particularly mentioned as a prerogative of sovereignty and is presumably not regarded as belonging to the crown exclusively. In his earlier work, Bodin was generally more considerate of local privilege.

35 The point of this discussion of the salt tax seems to be that it does not necessarily involve a sovereign monopoly of the right to mine it.

36 The right to seize whatever has been cast ashore from a wreck.

37 *Les mémoires et recherches* (in later editions entitled *Recueil des rois de France*) by Jean du Tillet (the elder) was published posthumously in 1577.

38 An early work of Bodin on public authority (*imperium*), perhaps going back to his days at the Law School of Toulouse. It was destroyed at his request when he died.

Book II, chapter 1

1 See above, p. 90, n.*

2 The harmonic proportion is a combination of the geometric and arithmetic series. It is called harmonic because it was closely associated with Pythagorean theories of music. Bodin is original as well as idiosyncratic in seeking to apply it to a synthesis of democratic and aristocratic ideas of policy and social justice. In *République* (1961), p. 1016, nn. 1–3 his example of the geometric series is 3–9–27–81; of the arithmetic 3–9–15–21–27; of the harmonic 4–6–8–12. In the harmonic proportion the quotient of the first term (4) divided by the third (8) is equal to the quotient (=½ in the illustration) arrived at by dividing the interval between the first and second terms (=2) by the interval between the third and fourth (=4) terms. It has also been pointed out to me by Matthew Franklin that one can look at a harmonic series in a way that makes the combination of the arithmetic and the geometric especially evident. Thus in a geometric series (e.g., 2–4–8–16–32–64) one can intercalate an equal (i.e., arithmetic) division in each of the intervals. Between 2 and 4 intercalate 3; between 4 and 8 intercalate 6; and so on. The result is the harmonic series 2–3–4–6–8–12–16–24–

32–48–64. Accounts of the harmonic proportion, its place in music theory, and some of Bodin's applications of it are Marocco Stuardi, "La teoria" and Villey, "Justice harmonique."

3 Bodin does not explain why he thought the Florentine "mixture" was nonetheless a species of democracy (in which only the more well-to-do inhabitants participated). He could have been thinking of the apparent power of the great council to control the other parts if it insisted, or else that any sharing of power among all three forms is *per se* democracy. Both arguments are given in the next paragraph but one.

4 An apparent reference to Machiavelli, Contarini, and More.

5 Bodin treats the Roman and other republican senates as basically analogous to royal privy councils.

6 As the marginal note in L181, D13 confirms, this refers to Du Haillan, Bernard de Girard, *De l'estat et succez des affaires de France* (Paris, 1571), in which Du Haillan follows the cautious formulation of Claude de Seyssel in *La monarchie de France* (1519). In part perhaps because of Bodin's criticism, Du Haillan carefully qualified his claim in the edition of 1580, although the change is not acknowledged by Bodin. See Church, *Constitutional Thought* (1965), pp. 121ff.

7 The peerage of France included the highest lords of the realm after the king. Originally twelve in number, by the sixteenth century it consisted only of six ecclesiastical peers and the count of Flanders who, however, stood outside the kingdom. The peers were technically members of the Parlement of Paris and constituted a special court within that body for hearing cases affecting the peers.

The assembly of all the officers refers to a kind of expanded version of the Parlement, called on an extraordinary basis, which included various ecclesiastics, representatives of the provincial Parlements, and representative *baillis* and *seneschaux*, among others.

8 A curious failure to consider Aristotle's recipes for mixture in *Politics*, Book IV, chapter 9.

9 But perhaps more accurately, Book IV, chapter 11, para. 19.

10 As McRae notes (192, A1), this probably refers to *Politics*, Book II, chapter 6, para. 16 where Aristotle is discussing Plato's *Laws*.

11 In the early republic, the equestrian order was the census group of substantial wealth that owed military service in the cavalry. In the later republic, it was the capitalist stratum of Roman society. Technically speaking, the eighteen equestrian centuries of the classical republic were alongside the first class rather than in it, as Bodin seems to have it.

12 Voting in the *comitia centuriata* was by centuries, the majority of centuries deciding. But since the centuries were based on wealth rather than number, the first class with 80 centuries and the equestrians with 18 had an absolute majority of the total of 193 centuries, and could thus decide the outcome if they were all in agreement. Roman procedure was to go from class to class until a majority of centuries was reached, at which point consultation ceased. Hence the lower classes not only had few chances to determine the outcome, but almost never got to voice their opinion.

13 Here again Bodin passes over those periods in which the Senate had a legislative veto.

Book II, chapter 5

1 Bodin is here adopting a basic distinction, used from the high Middle Ages up at least through Locke, between the tyrant without title, or usurper, on the one hand, who may be a person of virtue and good will, and a tyrant from malpractice on the other, who has come to power legitimately but persistently misuses it. Resistance to the first sort of tyrant was normally considered legitimate by the jurists and theologians, while resistance to the second sort was often condemned.

2 Bodin's list, given by IP, p. 609, n.a., includes, incorrectly it appears, St. Thomas Aquinas and Bartolus of Saxsoferrato, both of whom were more cautious than Bodin would seem to be suggesting.

3 The compound, "tyrant-king" or "king-tyrant," might suggest that a king whose title is otherwise legitimate could lose legitimacy through malpractice and thus become liable to resistance. Hence Bodin's objection to the term.

4 Bodin, no doubt lapsing inadvertently into the standard Roman formula (that is, *Senatus populusque Romanus*), here associates the Senate with the people in sovereignty, which is contrary to his theory of the Roman constitution.

5 Thus *Dig.* XLVIII, iv, 11 (which Bodin cites): "A person who dies while accused dies with his status intact since the crime is extinguished by his death, unless it is someone accused of *lèse majesté*, for unless he is cleared of the crime by his successors his estate is forfeited to the public treasury."

6 For inaccuracies in Bodin's account of the events surrounding the death of Conradin, see IP, pp. 627, n. 68 and 628, n. 70.

Index

CAMBRIDGE TEXTS IN THE HISTORY OF POLITICAL THOUGHT

Titles published in the series thus far

Aristotle *The Politics* (edited by Stephen Everson)
Bakunin *Statism and Anarchy* (edited by Marshall Shatz)
Bentham *A Fragment on Government* (introduction by Ross Harrison)
Bodin *On Sovereignty* (edited by Julian H. Franklin)
Bossuet *Politics Drawn from the Very Words of Holy Scripture* (edited by Patrick Riley)
Cicero *On Duties* (edited by M. T. Griffin and E. M. Atkins)
Constant *Political Writings* (edited by Biancamaria Fontana)
Filmer *Patriarcha and Other Writings* (edited by Johann P. Sommerville)
Hegel *Elements of the Philosophy of Right* (edited by Allen W. Wood and H. B. Nisbet)
Hobbes *Leviathan* (edited by Richard Tuck)
Hooker *Of the Laws of Ecclesiastical Polity* (edited by A. S. McGrade)
John of Salisbury *Policraticus* (edited by Cary Nederman)
Kant *Political Writings* (edited by H. S. Reiss and H. B. Nisbet)
Leibniz *Political Writings* (edited by Patrick Riley)
Locke *Two Treatises of Government* (edited by Peter Laslett)
Luther and Calvin on Secular Authority (edited by Harro Höpfl)
Machiavelli *The Prince* (edited by Quentin Skinner and Russell Price)
James Mill *Political Writings* (edited by Terence Ball)
J. S. Mill *On Liberty*, with *The Subjection of Women* and *Chapters on Socialism* (edited by Stefan Collini)
Milton *Political Writings* (edited by Martin Dzelzainis)
Montesquieu *The Spirit of the Laws* (edited by Anne M. Cohler, Basia Carolyn Miller and Harold Samuel Stone)
More *Utopia* (edited by George M. Logan and Robert M. Adams)
Nicholas of Cusa *The Catholic Concordance* (edited by Paul E. Sigmund)
Paine *Political Writings* (edited by Bruce Kuklick)
Pufendorf *On the Duty of Man and Citizen according to Natural Law* (edited by James Tully)
The Radical Reformation (edited by Michael G. Baylor)
Vitoria *Political Writings* (edited by Anthony Pagden and Jeremy Lawrance)
William of Ockham *A Short Discourse on Tyrannical Government* (edited by A. S. McGrade and John Kilcullen)